In memory of my beloved Marmie
and Dardie who shaped my life and
the lives of my five brothers
and sisters. They gave us the
love, confidence and
determination to succeed.

First published 2010 by Walker Books Ltd
87 Vauxhall Walk, London SE11 5HJ

2 4 6 8 10 9 7 5 3 1

Text © 2010 Floella Benjamin
Back cover image © Keith Taylor

The right of Floella Benjamin to be identified as author of this
work has been asserted by her in accordance with the
Copyright, Designs and Patents Act 1988

This book has been typeset in Ionic MT

Printed in Great Britain by Clays Ltd, St Ives plc

British Library Cataloguing in Publication Data:
a catalogue record for this book is
available from the British Library

ISBN 978-1-4063-0146-5

The Arms of Britannia

the teenage years of

Floella Benjamin

WALKER
BOOKS

CHAPTER ONE

I remember my first spiritual moment as if it were yesterday because it turned my life around. The experience affected my mind and my body and pierced deep into my soul. Looking back, I suppose it came at a crucial point in my life; any later, who knows what might have been.

It was September 1964 and I had been in England, the land I had loved from afar, for four years now. That love had faded rapidly as I began to view my new homeland with increasing trepidation. The Land of Hope and Glory, Mother of the Free, had not quite lived up to its name. My father, who we called Dardie, had uprooted the family from our home in Trinidad, our secure Caribbean island in the sun, to bring us to the Motherland, but I had found little comfort in the arms of Britannia.

I was now fourteen, and during those first four years in Britain I had developed into a person I didn't like, a tormented, tortured being, full of fear, anxiety and hatred, which was almost too much for a young girl to bear. For no good reason I could imagine, this torment had been thrust upon me by insensitive, cruel, ignorant people. So, as a matter of survival, the hard vicious side of me grew stronger and stronger each day. Intense emotions followed me as I slammed the front door of my home behind me and left my comfort zone, the security of my loving family, stepping out of the protection of my mother, Marmie, who cloaked me with confidence and love.

Despite being exposed to all this love, so essential for a child's well-being, my heart would lurch inside me, pounding with deafening pressure. My sweating palms felt like dampened, sodden soil, aching as I clenched my fists tight.

My eyes would scan wildly across the urban horizon for the enemy, never sure when or where they would spring from to attack me with their venomous tongues. The lash of their words would be an instant trigger for me to react. I was constantly prepared for action, like a soldier on patrol.

My tears had all but dried up, for I had cried into my pillow night after night for four years. I never thought I would be crying in England, not like I had during the days and nights in Trinidad when I was separated from my family. Marmie and Dardie had gone ahead to England, taking my younger siblings Cynthia and Junior with them. They had left my sister Sandra and me with one foster family, and my brothers Lester and Ellington with another.

That miserable period of my life away from my beloved family had only lasted just over a year, but the feeling of separation and insecurity took its toll, and salty tears soaked my pillow each and every one of those unhappy nights in Trinidad. Yet now I was in England I still felt as if I was in a sandy desert looking for an oasis where I could quench my sorrowful thirst.

Sandra and I would talk of running away and escaping back to Trinidad. But what would we be returning to? There was no going back. Marmie and Dardie had sold all our possessions. Our home, the small whitewashed house on stilts, was no longer ours and we certainly didn't have the money for the return passage. I just had to stick it out. But how long could I continue to carry this burden of rejection that was driving me crazy with rage?

I tried to suppress the violent emotions stirring inside me, but it didn't take much to make them rise to the surface. For as I walked the streets of London, which back in Trinidad we were told were paved with gold, the streets which I thought would be welcoming, I found only fear and very little comfort. I was never quite sure who would call me a nasty name, who was going to spit at me or which grown man was going to lift up my skirt and sneer, "Where's your tail then, monkey?"

On one particular occasion, as Sandra and I innocently stood on a railway station platform, a train drew in. To our horror, some men pulled down their carriage window, opened their flies, took aim and tried to pee on us. Fortunately we were ready for any unexpected attacks and avoided the repulsive spray. But the men's laughter rang in my ears, and this sickening offence was added to the endless catalogue of assaults and indignities which fuelled my anger and served only to make me more vicious.

My brother Lester, the most handsome, sweet, shy little boy who would never hurt a fly, bore the brunt of the attacks from bullying thugs. They took great delight in shedding his blood by giving him a bashed nose or a cut lip. One day I witnessed a gang of bullies laying into his defenceless body, his white shirt covered in blood, as he helplessly and unsuccessfully tried to protect himself.

The injustice propelled me at them and, when they saw the ferocity that was in my soul, they turned tail and ran for their lives. But that day I had a force and power within me that made me hunt them down like a cheetah. One by one I caught them and they felt the intensity of my anger as I thumped them to the ground, trying to pound their prejudices out of them.

These incidents were not few and far between; they were relentless. I never knew when I would need to turn into an Incredible Hulk of a being to defend myself or my brothers and sisters.

Shamefully, I was almost beginning to enjoy making people suffer the blows of my fists or the pain of anything I could get my hands on to strike them down with. Whenever an attacker came towards me, my thought process would be, "Are they going to call me a name? Are they going to pelt me with something? What are they going to do to abuse me?" If an attack didn't materialize, my aching heart would ease temporarily. I would sigh with relief – but be instantly ready as the next person approached me. I had made up my mind that this was the only way to survive in England.

Then, like a bolt from the blue, came what I can only describe as a spiritual moment which transformed me.

Marmie had given me a shopping list and I was on my way to the shops in Penge High Street near where we lived in Anerley, south London. I knew I might have to face the indignity of being ignored by the shop assistants, as though I was invisible. I had grown accustomed to that, but I had to hold my ground and wait until they got the message that I was not going to leave until I got served. Facing Marmie without the shopping was not an option; she would have only made me go back.

So, armed with my list and physical power, and ready for the enemy, I headed down Anerley Hill. No sooner had I left my secure base camp than I had my first encounter, in the form of a boy about my age, sucking a lollipop, coming towards me up the hill. As he got near he spat

the usual hateful words at me, abusing my existence, insulting me and condemning my colour. I
smiled with delight; he was easy prey. He didn't
realize what he was letting himself in for.

The Incredible Hulk within me stirred and
came out with explosive force.

I didn't want it to be this way. I wanted to
be accepted, appreciated. I wanted to feel as
though I belonged, as though I was part of British society. I didn't want to be seen as an enemy,
but as a friend who loved this great nation.
The heartache was even further compounded
by the hypocrisy of our local church, where we
were told in no uncertain terms that we weren't
accepted.

Why couldn't it be the way we'd been indoc-
trinated to believe it would be in this land when
I was at school in Trinidad? Why weren't the
streets paved with a golden welcome?

I looked at the boy's ugly face as he sucked
his lollipop and jeered at me. Faces always look
ugly when people are being nasty and wicked.
My anger grew to a crescendo as I stared back
at him. I had the upper hand because I was going
down the hill and had the full force of gravity
behind me. We were now face to face but he still
didn't realize that he had aroused the monster
within me.

With lightning speed, I pushed the lollipop
down his throat as hard as I could. "Let that be

a lesson to you," I thought with glee. He began to choke, the smile now wiped off his sallow face. He started gasping for air and began to turn blue as I pushed the lollipop even harder.

Suddenly the world seemed to stand still. There was a silence and my whole body became light as though it was suspended in time and space. I felt a pure, cool, calming feeling flowing through my veins.

Then I heard a soft gentle voice calling my name with love and affection, the way I wanted people to speak to me. I listened in silence, spellbound like a moth fluttering in the light of a glowing candle.

Repeatedly the voice chanted my name: "Floella, Floella, Floella, what are you doing? Because of this boy's stupidity, his ignorance and prejudices, you are going to get yourself into deep trouble. Stop it, stop it now! You know who you are, you know you are loved by your five brothers and sisters, your mother and father. Are you prepared to bring shame on them all by committing this vicious act?

"Be proud of who you are, and if anyone has a problem with your colour then it's their problem, not yours. Don't let others poison your soul. Let their prejudices bounce off your self-worth and high self-esteem because if you continue to behave this way you will be confirming their perception of you. You were created the way you are, and nothing can change that. So use the force of your mind to set you free and drive you forward to your rightful place. Floella, you must hold your head up high and use your strength and power in a positive way, now and always."

At that moment I felt as though the toughened coat that had encased my heart had shattered like ice and slowly melted away. All the feelings of anger, bitterness, hatred and fear had disappeared. I began to breathe with ease and felt as though a joyful, protective blanket had been wrapped around me.

I was shocked back to reality by the desperate choking sounds of the boy, who by this time was fighting for survival.

I swiftly plucked the lollipop from his throat, giving him back his air supply, and said with a smile, "Yes, I know who I am and I'm proud."

He looked at me in dismay as he took great gulps of air. Then, his eyes wide with relief and astonishment, he wandered off. I wanted to embrace him to show my gratitude, for he had done me a huge favour that day. He had freed my unhappy soul from its chains of misery.

For now I was happily on a path that I felt would take me to my destiny. That was the day I started fighting with my brains and not my fists. I skipped down the hill clutching my shopping list, laughing and singing with joy, smiling with happiness, hoping the feeling would last.

CHAPTER TWO

From as far back as I can remember, Dardie had always told us stories which I suppose were a legacy he was passing down to us about who we were and our heritage. He was a visionary. "In order to know your future you have to know your past, your history," he would say during those hours of storytelling, his voice taking on the tone of a great philosopher. "But it must not inhibit you from moving forward freely, unburdened by the shackles of your past."

Now, after my spiritual moment, I was slowly beginning to understand what he meant, and the significance of those words of wisdom. He told us so much about our history and our culture, laying a lasting foundation for me to build on. That began with his storytelling, which he was great at.

The exciting stories he told us when we were little children back in Trinidad were so vivid I wanted to live them and be one of the characters. They ranged from fantastic African Anansi stories to historical stories to stories about movie stars. I was never sure if he was making them up or not, but I didn't care because they fired up my imagination.

Dardie was one of fifteen children and was born in Antigua, the son of Leonard Benjamin, a third-generation freed enslaved man. Dardie's mother died in childbirth when he was four, so he was brought up by his father, my grandfather, who I never met. In fact, I never knew any of my grandparents, as both Marmie's parents had died by the time she was eleven. But I felt as if I knew Grandad Leonard intimately because of the stories we were repeatedly told about him.

Grandad Leonard was a tailor by trade and he made uniforms for the police force, prison officers and soldiers of Antigua. But he was also a human-rights activist, as he felt there was great injustice in the way the Antiguan people were treated by their British Colonial masters. At that time Antigua was part of the British Empire, and it remained so until 1981 when it gained independence. From 1967 until today it has remained part of the Commonwealth, the organization that keeps millions of people across every continent together with a common bond. Grandad Leonard tried to get the workers to form a union and was having so much success that, in order to avoid a rebellion, the British Government sent a delegate to Antigua to hold discussions with my grandfather and his associates. The results of this meeting led to the formation of the Antiguan Trades and Labour Union.

Even though Dardie was a boy when this happened, he took after his father when it came to union and human-rights activity. Years later, when he left Antigua for Trinidad where he met and married Marmie, he too was heavily involved in the union movement at the oil refinery in Point-à-Pierre, where he worked as a field policeman.

Grandad Leonard also had a stint in politics, but not for very long because most of his lucrative contracts were for the Government. In order to stay in politics he had to surrender the trade which brought in his finances and, because of this predicament he eventually had to give up his political ambitions and return to tailoring.

But that was just one side of him. Grandad Leonard had an Achilles' heel – a weakness for "the ladies" and several of them mothered his fifteen children. He never lost his taste for women right up to the end of his life. He even wanted to make love to his nurse while on his deathbed.

By that time he had frittered away the fortune left to him by his father, my great-grandfather, a rich merchant who had made a fortune through trading produce. He had a fleet of schooners, which took cargo between the islands near Antigua and Barbuda. He himself was born on the island of Barbuda, just off the coast of Antigua. Barbuda was left to the islanders by the British Codrington family, who had leased it for "one fat sheep" from the British Government in the seventeenth century.

The Codringtons, who had owned Barbuda for almost two hundred years, decreed that anyone born on the island or who had Barbudian blood could inherit the land. They could never buy it and own it outright, but they could claim a patch of land and live on it. This means that I can always go back and stake my claim there if I so wish, because I am a blood offspring of one of the islanders.

There is a legend that Barbuda was used to breed slaves to sell to plantation owners on other islands. But no one will ever know for sure if this is true. My great-grandfather was the son of a nineteenth-century freed enslaved man who was taught a trade even before the end of slavery, for, although the majority of enslaved people worked in the sugar fields, many were encouraged to become tradesmen and -women. This was because a variety of trades were needed to service the vast plantations and the lucrative sugar trade. Work as blacksmiths, carpenters, stonemasons, tailors, boatmen and shipwrights were just some of the trades Africans who were brought to the islands were required to undertake.

After the abolition of slavery, however, these people's livelihood started to disappear, as the sugar trade went into decline and they were no longer needed to supply goods or services to the plantations, neither to those who worked on them nor to those who owned them. It became a very difficult time for these traders because, rather than give the land to the freed African enslaved people, the plantation owners brought in indentured workers from India, China and even Europe. They offered plots of land as payment to these new workers, who had to work a five- to seven-year contract before they could claim their land.

So my great-grandfather was fortunate to have secured a successful business, which continued to thrive after the abolition of slavery. This was because of his drive, tenacity, determination and entrepreneurial skills – qualities the millions of African enslaved people had developed during their two hundred years of repression.

I can only imagine what they must have felt like during those barbaric and brutal days. I thought my treatment on my arrival in Britain was bad, but it can have been nothing compared with the pain, suffering and indignity endured by enslaved men, women and children.

Their journey from Africa started with a rude awakening. Millions of them were taken from their homes and villages, often in the middle of the night, shackled and marched to the specially-built forts on the west coast of Africa, which became known as the Gold Coast because of this lucrative trade in humans. If the captives weren't strong they didn't survive; they were dead and gone.

Those who did survive were branded on the chest by their captors and confined in a caged pit, sometimes for months, to wait for the ships to take them thousands of miles across the Atlantic Ocean to a strange land.

If they weren't strong, they too were dead and gone. The journey would take three to four months, with them packed into the ship's hold like sardines in a tin. The stench of seasickness, of vomit, urine and faeces, was like being plunged into the pit of hell. If anyone got too ill, their journey would end abruptly – they would be hurled into the ocean waves and washed into oblivion.

Only the very strongest survived.

I thought my four days of seasickness during the two weeks of my four-thousand-mile journey by ship across the Atlantic from Trinidad to Britain was unbearable. I wonder if I could have survived the journey of my ancestors.

When they arrived in the Caribbean, they were made to look respectable and saleable by having gunpowder rubbed into their wounds to disguise them. The pain must have been excruciating. But they had to look presentable in order to get a good price from those who were to be their new masters.

All family ties were extinguished. Mothers, children, fathers, cousins were all separated and condemned to various islands across the

Caribbean. Once sold to the highest bidder, they were again branded on the chest by their new owners and put to work in the plantation fields, forbidden to speak in their native tongue, practise their religion or retain their culture. Even their birth names were eliminated, wiped out for ever, and instead they were given the name of whoever owned them.

If anyone rebelled they were brutally dealt with. To some plantation owners an African life was cheap and the death of an enslaved being was a form of amusement.

Many of the millions of enslaved people did rebel and were prepared to die for their freedom. Dardie told us of a mysterious place in Antigua called Devil's Bridge, on the east coast of the island, which drew many enslaved people to it. Unlike the densely forested and mountainous islands of Jamaica, Dominica, Grenada and St Lucia, Antigua was relatively flat and there were virtually no hiding-places for anyone to escape the brutality. Legend told of how, during the days of slavery, many Africans used to go to Devil's Bridge and call to the ocean to take them, before hurling themselves into the raging jaws of the Atlantic. They believed they would be returned by the sea to Africa, their homeland.

Another story Dardie used to tell us was of the Antiguan gunpowder plot, of how the rebel Prince Klass, who was also known as King Court, plotted to blow up all the plantation owners at a ball they were going to attend. But someone betrayed him and his eighty-eight accomplices, and they were all caught and brutally executed. King Court himself was beheaded, his body was burned and his head left on the jail door for all to see as a deterrent to anyone plotting rebellion.

To have survived all the adversities during that period meant you would have faced the worst atrocities. If you weren't strong, you were dead and gone.

To me, Dardie's stories meant I was a survivor from strong stock, and as a Caribbean descendant I had a duty to make my ancestors proud, to make their journey worthwhile and meaningful. They had paved the way for future generations. I had to travel the path they had secured for me. The responsibility I had was to live their dream. It was going to be a hard and traumatic journey, but to reach my destination successfully I would have to channel my anger and frustration at the injustice I had received in a positive way, without resentment or vengefulness. Of this I had to keep reminding myself.

CHAPTER THREE

Being one of six children had the effect of making me very competitive. At home we would constantly try to outdo one another when it came to achieving. "Education is your passport to life," Marmie would drum into us each day. This would go round and round in my head, relentlessly driving me on to accomplish my goals. So at the run-up to the end of the school year, at exam time, things got serious and we knuckled down and studied to see who could get the highest grades.

Sandra was the eldest, so had the added responsibility – burden, I suppose – of looking after the rest of us when Marmie and Dardie went out to work to make sure we had enough money to live on.

Dardie sometimes worked as a mechanic, but mostly he went away to play jazz, often abroad. That was his main reason for leaving Trinidad in the first place. Originally he had wanted to take us to America. "New York is the home of jazz," he used to say with a tone of adventure and excitement in his voice. But Grandad Leonard, who left Antigua and lived in New York for a while, told him not to emigrate to America with six children. He told Dardie that England was a much better place for children, and reluctantly Dardie took his advice.

I often wonder how my life would have turned out if we had gone to America instead. For one thing, I would have got the chance to meet Grandad Leonard. I did see a picture of him, though; he looked like an African emperor, with a certain regality about him.

He reminded me of my youngest sister, Cynthia, who walked like a gazelle, tall, statuesque and elegant.

Marmie was a natural childminder, so to earn money she cared for babies during the day at our house. Having six children of her own made nurturing come easily to her. During the evening she also used to work in a laundry – but that wasn't all: altogether she had three jobs. The third was cleaning offices in Victoria in the early mornings. I used to go there with her during the school holidays. It was exciting to be in the huge office building with phalanxes of empty desks lined up between rows of pillars. There was always an eerie silence about the open-plan work arena and I would try to imagine myself sitting behind one of those desks.

I didn't want to end up cleaning someone else's mess or scrubbing toilets. But it had to be done at that time, and helping Marmie wasn't a chore, it was a necessity. The money was going to put food in our bellies, glorious food, wholesome food, which she took delight in showing us how to cook. My passion for cooking still remains.

In those days there was very little wastage. And in the winter months when fruit was scarce and expensive there was very little extravagance. But Marmie made sure we still had our daily intake of fresh fruit and vegetables although we did have to share one apple between all six of us – and everything was eaten, pips and all.

On Friday evenings, on her way back home from the laundry, Marmie would stop to buy us sweets as a treat. My favourite was nut brittle – nuts covered in hard caramel. I used to love going to the sweetshop myself to see all the jars full of tempting delights, but having Marmie bring the sugary treats home in paper bags was just as exciting.

One Friday evening at the end of the summer term we were as excited as ever to see her come through the door with our treats. She always looked tired after the long week of hard toil, but she never lost her smile and dressed with style as though she owned the business. Marmie always had a sense of pride about her – she was doing what she had to do, and made personal sacrifices in order for her children to have a bright future.

We flocked around her as she sat down, the noise of our excitement filling the air with expectation. She handed out our treats one by one, and we contained our boisterousness by politely thanking her for them. We could see how happy that made her.

On this particular evening we were more excited than ever, because we had brought home our school reports and were anxious to hear the results of all our efforts. Who was going to get the best grades this time and to make Marmie proud?

We had left our reports unopened on the table for her to read. That was a way of showing respect to her. Sandra's was the first to be opened. Marmie read it for a moment and started to cry. Then she looked up and said, "Sandra, come here."

Sandra, who was busy getting Marmie's evening meal ready, walked slowly over to her and said, " Yes, Marmie?"

"Do you know what this report says about you, Sandra?" asked Marmie, her voice trembling with emotion.

Sandra stood there and shook her head. In a little voice that seemed to come from far away, she whispered, "No."

We all hushed, the competitiveness leaving our hearts, the anticipation of hearing our results dying as we realized something was wrong.

"You have come second to last in the class, Sandra," said Marmie, "and it's my fault. I have left too many responsibilities on your shoulders. You have had to neglect your homework in order to look after your brothers and sisters.

Next week I am going to hand in my notice at the laundry and make sure I am here in the evenings so that you can get on with your homework. We will have to manage on what money we have."

That meant we would no longer have our Friday-night sweetie treats when Marmie came home, but that was a small price to pay for Sandra getting back to the top of the form.

CHAPTER FOUR

We all loved going to school, and shone in different ways. Sandra soon caught up with her peers again and excelled in science and English. Lester loved maths and could rattle off his times tables as quick as a flash. Cynthia was great at drawing. She came to England with Marmie when she was two, and when we were all reunited as a family she gave us a collection of paintings and drawings she had done for us, with a full explanation of every detail in her creations. Later she took up music too and became a brilliant classical pianist. Come to think of it, she was good at anything she turned her hand to.

Roy, who we called Junior because he was named after Dardie, was always a genius, far cleverer than the rest of us academically. He was put in classes with older children all through his school years as he was ahead of his age group. But when it came to taking his eleven plus, the school lied to Marmie and said he had failed. Actually they never even let him take the exam. We realized it was because they knew boys from his background were rarely accepted at grammar schools in the area where we lived. But Junior did go on to gain his Master's by the time he was twenty-two and eventually went on to work for the IT company that developed the bar code.

Ellington was a law unto himself. He was excellent at maths and solving problems, and he became a quantity surveyor and later a property developer. He was also a great wheeler dealer, a people person. Mind you, he and I used to fight continually and neither of us liked losing. I usually won our spats because I was older – until one day he punched me in the stomach so hard it winded me. I realized then that he was getting stronger than me, and we called a truce, but only after he was reprimanded by Marmie for punching a girl so hard.

I was what you might call a "Jill of all trades". I loved school and took part in practically everything. I was proud to sing in the choir and my music teacher used to say I had a way of smiling while I sang. But she told the other girls to copy me, which is the worst thing a teacher can do because it made some of them quite jealous.

I loved taking part and competing in all sports and I was in the thick of it when it came to hockey, netball and running, as well as tennis (although I was asked to give up tennis as I hit the ball so hard no one could return it!).

The only sport I didn't excel in was swimming because my confidence was badly damaged by the teacher who told me condescendingly, "Coloured people can't swim so you don't have to try." I think she meant well, and really believed the myth that people of my race had an extra bone in each foot which prevented us from swimming, but the ignorance at that time was damaging to the soul and stifled my potential. I still can't swim to this day.

But no one could hold me back on the sports field. When I eventually worked my way up to become the school's sports captain, I looked forward to taking the Championship Cup home for the weekend. This was a school tradition that I had seen take place over my years there, so I couldn't wait for my turn to have that privilege bestowed upon me after having led the school teams to many triumphs over the years.

But when that momentous time came, I was stunned by the teacher's action. She very politely, but firmly, took the silver chalice out of my hand and said, "I'll look after that for you, Floella."

I felt the sting of tears in my eyes, but I didn't let them flow as I speechlessly watched her walk away with the cup. The anger rose up inside me, almost erupting through my disappointment and disbelief, but I was determined that her action was not going to destroy my spirit and self-worth, and Marmie and the rest of my family gave me the strength to get through it.

At school I kept on smiling and never showed any anger to my teachers. I was going to be a winner and I had to prove to myself that I could endure whatever was thrown at me. My reward was that I allowed myself to experience the significant privileges that the school offered me. Had I reacted in a negative way, I would not have had any of those opportunities.

One of the opportunities I felt blessed to have was when my music teacher arranged for the choir to attend the orchestral rehearsals at the Festival Hall on London's South Bank on Saturday mornings. This opened my eyes to a type of music I would have never discovered by myself, and hearing the orchestra play classical music took me to another dimension.

Another exciting trip was the one to see the Royal Tournament at Earls Court, where teams from the Army, Navy and Air Force put on a spectacular show of military prowess and daring precision. This was the reward given to a group of girls who were high achievers during the school year because we too had shown team spirit, as well as physical and mental strength. The hour-long coach trip to west London was part of the excitement, and the prize seat was the one at the back of the coach where we would wave at the motorists behind us. I went on several of these trips (and it was always guaranteed that someone would be sick on the coach).

The thrill of seeing the competitiveness of the teams in the big arena, the smell of the horses, tinged with the smell of grease and oil from the machines, made my imagination run wild. I would watch the spectacle with delight, and I especially loved the precision of the two teams as they took their heavy field guns apart and carried them piece by piece on their shoulders from one end of the arena to the other, before reassembling them. We would shout until we were hoarse for our chosen team. The winning team would be the first to fire their gun with a deafening bang, which always made me jump out of my seat, shrieking with laughter and excitement. I really wanted to be part of one of those teams, and even had fleeting thoughts of joining the Army so I could compete there one day. But those thoughts were soon forgotten when I left Earls Court on the return journey, exhausted but happy.

Mrs Thomas, my English teacher, also gave me opportunities to widen my horizons. She had an aristocratic air about her – and she taught me a hard but important lesson on the day she called me a guttersnipe and told me to drop my sweet Trinidadian accent. "If you want to remain in my class you will learn to speak the Queen's English," she haughtily instructed me.

I desperately wanted to be accepted by the girls at school and feel as though I belonged, so I deliberately used to exaggerate my Trinidadian accent to make them laugh. I didn't realize they were laughing at me, not with me, and saw me as a joker. So when Mrs Thomas told me drop my accent – in front of the whole class, while I was reading out a poem in her lesson – I felt as though she was stripping away the one thing that made me feel special among the girls. Fortunately, Marmie wisely sided with Mrs Thomas and told me to obey orders. Had I not done so, I would have been put into a class for children with learning difficulties, because the teachers would claim they didn't understand what I said, so I must be stupid.

That is what happened to other Caribbean girls whose parents didn't take the same line as Marmie. I didn't completely discard my beautiful Trinidadian lilt – I still have it as part of my heritage – but the "Queen's English" accent gave me depth, broadened my mind, my communication skills and my capabilities. I learnt almost overnight to adapt, and to embrace any situation in which I found myself.

Just over a year after the dressing-down Mrs Thomas gave me, I stood in the control tower at Heathrow Airport, marvelling at the huge, revolutionary new computer that had been installed, and I smiled to myself. I was there because of Mrs Thomas, who now saw me as a conscientious pupil since I showed passion for my work and spoke with the clarity she had insisted upon. I felt privileged to have been chosen by her to go on this special visit. Her husband, who worked at the control tower, had invited us to see what at that time was an incredible sight.

But for me it went beyond that. It meant I was learning to be a winner and to take advantage of every opportunity that presented itself, as this would make me a well-rounded person and I would benefit from those precious experiences later on. Had I not had them, I would have been the loser.

CHAPTER FIVE

The sibling competitiveness that ran through the veins of our family bonded us together so tightly we didn't need any outside influences. But sometimes we did do rather foolish things in our desire to get one up on each other, and during the Christmas festive season this was no different.

Marmie always made Christmas one of the most special and memorable times for us. She prepared the dried fruits for the Christmas cake months before. Raisins, sultanas and currants were soaked in rum and left in a tall glass jar to mature and marinate, before being used to make the dark, moist, rich Caribbean cake, full of nuts and cherries too.

It took a whole day to make the delicious cake. The first stage of the process was the whipping of the butter and sugar by hand into a creamy mixture. This was not something I liked doing and I would try to find an excuse to stop after a few moments. Sandra usually drew the short straw and did most of the hard work. I didn't mind cracking open the eggs, though, making sure no eggshell got in the bowl. The eggs had to be cracked over a separate bowl in case any of them was rotten. The smell of rotten eggs would put you off food for days. The adding of the eggs into the buttery, creamy mixture was very satisfying, as the two textures blended together to form the base for the other ingredients.

This was where Marmie took over. She would vigorously sieve the flour into the mixing bowl like an experienced supervisor, administering her magical touch of authority. The spices – ginger, nutmeg and cinnamon – would be added with a flourish, together with the vanilla essence. She would then give the command to dust the cherries with flour, and stand by for the big moment. The tall glass jar containing the soaked fruits would be ceremonially opened and the powerful fumes of the alcohol would assail our senses.

The swollen, soaked fruits that had been engulfed in rum, hidden away in a dark corner for months, were now exposed to the world in their full glory. There was a feeling of excitement as the hundreds of dark juicy fruits tumbled into the large mixing bowl, splashing the sides and leaving their trails behind them.

The quality of the finished cake would be judged by the moistness of the fruits, so this was the most important part of creating the *pièce de résistance*.

After the nuts and cherries, which had been floured to stop them sinking to the bottom of the cake, were added, we would each take a turn to stir the mixture and make a wish. This was a family tradition and it had to be done. I never wished for toys, as Marmie didn't believe in wasting money on things that would soon be broken or destroyed. I just wished to be happy.

The mixture would then be poured into the greased and floured cake tin and carefully placed into the heated oven to be baked for hours. I used to imagine music being played and a choir singing as the cake went on its journey into the furnace of fire which slowly cooked the most important part of our traditional Christmas feast.

This ritual was a reminder of our Caribbean culture, which was very much based on British traditions. In Trinidad we didn't have snow or Christmas trees, but we did see those images on Christmas cards which were imported from Britain.

To me, the star of the cards was Father Christmas. I used to think he looked so jolly and kind, his cheeks so rosy and round, his fluffy white beard so soft, the redness of his coat – bright and flaming like a robin's breast – standing out against the snowy backdrop. When I finally met him in Santa's Grotto in Selfridges on Oxford Street, I wasn't disappointed. He was everything I had imagined him to be.

Each year at Christmas time Marmie would take us on a pilgrimage to the West End of London to see the towering Christmas tree in Trafalgar Square, the glittering lights in Regent Street and finally to meet my beloved Santa.

One year, on our way there, it snowed so heavily that the bus we were on ground to a halt, and to our horror we had to get off and walk back home, our great expectations of meeting our Christmas icon melting away in a moment. But at least it was snowing, and I loved being in the magical surroundings of the crispy, white wonderland which made London look just like a Christmas card.

Carol-singers also featured on the Christmas cards we saw back in Trinidad, but in Britain carol-singing was something we did at home, not in church. Our experience of being told we were not welcome in church when we did attend didn't put us off celebrating our religious beliefs. I loved singing the carols on Christmas Eve after all the hard work of preparation had been completed.

Christmas morning was the most exciting time of the year. The table would be laden for a feast. Cooked ham covered in cloves gave off a pungent smell, mixed with the smell of freshly baked bread. Marmie never forgot the piccalilli – no self-respecting mother would ever do that.

Prayers would be said before we ate, and

then the feast began. All day was spent eating. Turkey was, of course, on the menu, but cooked the Caribbean way, seasoned with exotic herbs and spices and left to marinate overnight before being roasted till it was golden brown.

Playing games and having fun was also part of our traditional activities during the festive season and allowed our competitiveness to shine. One by one we would take turns to do our party piece, singing, dancing or telling a story.

Then, finally, came the moment we had all been excitedly waiting for – the sharing out of the Christmas cake. It would be ceremonially brought out by Marmie. "Well, here it is," she would proudly say. "I hope you all like it."

Dardie would take a knife to cut the first slice and give his verdict. He would bury the knife slowly into the thick dark cake, cutting through the moistened fruit. Then he would smell the slice and take in a whiff of the rum, more of which had been poured over the cake when it came out of the oven to be rested. "Mmm, it looks good and smells great," he would say with a smile. Marmie would look on with pride as we all waited with bated breath. "And it tastes good too," he would announce as he took a mouthful. A cheer would go up and we would all clamour for a slice of Marmie's rich fruity cake.

The next family tradition was passing around

the bowl of mixed nuts. This was the time to show off and compete for the title of Nutcracker of the Season. We didn't have a nutcracker so we had to use a hammer or pliers instead. But as we were all so anxious to crack open our nuts, having to wait for an implement was too much to bear. We had to think of other ways of cracking the shells and getting to the nuts inside.

The Brazil nut had the hardest shell, then the almond, next the hazelnut and least challenging the walnut, because two walnuts could easily be crushed together by hand to crack them open. I remember thinking a great way to get to the nuts quickly would be to crack them open with my teeth. I had a wide mouth, a strong jaw and large molars where a nut could nestle comfortably. My brothers and sisters thought this was a great idea, but they didn't have quite such strong jaws as mine – except for Sandra, that is. She and I were best at cracking, and that was how the challenge for the title Nutcracker of the Season started.

We would put the nuts into the side of our mouths and crunch down on them as hard as we could. The person who could crack the most nuts would be the winner. I think Sandra won the title more times than I did in the end, because after a few years I had to retire due to the fact that I had damaged the enamel coating on my teeth. This meant I had to visit the dentist for repairs, which was one of the most torturous experiences for me.

Not only had I damaged my teeth with my nut-cracking, but tooth decay had also set in because I had smuggled sweets into my bedroom, put them under my pillow and secretly and foolishly sucked them when I went to bed at night after I had brushed my teeth. This carried on over a long period until finally tooth decay meant I had to reluctantly face the dentist's drill.

I remember sitting in the chair of the executioner – that's how I saw the dentist. Her face was covered with a mask, only her eyes were visible and they seemed to smile with glee. Her silver implements were laid out ready to be used for the torture. I can't remember being given any pain-killers; my body, my senses were all too numb for me to remember. But the sound of the drill seemed to amplify in my head.

"Open wide and stay still," her muffled voice said.

Then she put the drill in my mouth and dug as though she was searching for gold. I held my breath, waiting for the unwelcome but necessary exploration to finish. I must have fainted, because the next thing I knew I was spitting out pink liquid with pieces of silver filling in it. My mouth felt like a boxer's after a ten-round

41

heavyweight fight, and my lips were so numb I couldn't feel them as I wiped away the dribble running uncontrollably down my chin.

My foolish behaviour had caused me unnecessary pain and I gladly handed over the mantle of Nutcracker of the Season to Sandra.

We did eventually get a nutcracker and stopped using our teeth. But the rest of our Christmas traditions carried on as always. I still love Christmas and do the same things with my family even today. Except for the nutcracker competition, that is.

CHAPTER SIX

After my spiritual encounter I started to develop a contented feeling in my heart that always brought a smile to my face. I felt as though I was slowly becoming aware of who I really was and what life meant to me. But I wasn't quite sure of how I could get the most out of it. Certain things began to happen, and instead of just allowing them to flow by me, I seized on them because all the pieces of my life's jigsaw were slowly falling into place, forming the map that would help me to reach the right destination. They added up to make a big picture in my head.

Looking back, I can see that it all really started after my successful performance at the school concert in which I had given my all. I had sung with such force and conviction that I had changed people's perception of me. That's when I truly began to discover what it would take to move on and get others to see who I really was, not just see my colour and dismiss me. It meant I had to work doubly hard to have any chance of being taken seriously. On my journey to my destiny I had to reach for the sky in earnest, never taking my foot off the pedal of life. It's an exhausting burden to be judged simply by the colour of your skin, but I had to rise above it and prove myself.

So I started to work twice as hard at school

and I began to see my teachers as my best friends. They had the gift I needed in order to succeed. The the gift of education. Even if I didn't like the way they presented it to me, it didn't matter. I had to accept the precious gift with grace and humility. I had to see them not as enemies but as providers of knowledge, which I in turn could use to the best of my ability.

I was like a plant extracting the nutrients of knowledge they were feeding me, and each time I mastered the art of drawing out and understanding what I was being taught I felt so good, like a sprinter pushing herself forward to break the tape at the end of a race.

But having a recurring dream didn't help the situation. In the dream I would be running up a hill as fast as I could. I was being chased by someone or something but I was never quite sure what it was. I would get to the top of the hill, only to find there was a sheer drop into the ocean. So in order to escape my pursuers, I would have to jump off the cliff. But every time I jumped I would wake up mid-fall, just before I hit the rocks below. I was never caught, nor did I come to a sorry end and get wiped out, because I would force myself back to sleep to dream of a happy ending and win the chase each time. The positive side of my nature refused to let me be beaten.

I kept this recurring anxiety dream secret

and never shared it with anyone, as I was afraid to expose my vulnerability. It took its time to disappear altogether, but it was beginning to occur less frequently. However, occasionally it would still show itself in full glorious Technicolor.

I must have exuded a positive attitude and a certain confidence, because the other girls at school started to come to me for advice and motivation.

One particular girl who did so was from Jamaica. She was one of the few other West Indians in the school. She, like me, was left in the Caribbean by her parents when she was four. But the difference between us was that she wasn't reunited with them for ten years. Sadly and traumatically for her, when she came to Britain to live with them she felt like a stranger. Her mother, who was now married to someone else, had started another family, so she now had younger half-brothers and -sisters who she had to get to know. She was jealous of them because they knew they were loved and were not left with someone else to be looked after. This girl never felt as though she fitted in anywhere until she came to my house.

I too had been left by my parents, but only for fifteen months. Even so, that feeling of separation always stayed with me, despite the fact Marmie made it easier to bear when we all got back together by coating us with love and affection.

The foster parents she had left us with in Trinidad were the wickedest of people. We had to call them Auntie and Uncle, but they seemed to take delight in mistreating us physically as well as psychologically. Marmie and Dardie hadn't done anything unusual in leaving us behind. During that time it was customary for children to be left with family and friends when their parents went to Britain to start a new life, and help rebuild the Motherland after the destruction of World War Two. The decision by countless parents to move to Britain came as a bombshell to the thousands of children who were left behind. They had no say in this devastating, life-changing catastrophe. They just had to accept it.

When I brought my Jamaican friend round to my house she started to cry, as she wanted so much to be part of our strong family unit. Marmie always treated her with a certain tenderness, as though she wanted to take away her pain.

My friend was one of many Caribbeans who were emotionally damaged by being left behind for too long by their parents, and many of them suffered in silence and never spoke about the pain they carried hidden at the back of their broken hearts. Her family moved away and I lost touch with her so I never knew whether her emotional scars ever healed.

My best friend at school, however, was a girl who could only be described as an English rose. Her name was Janice. She had long, straight, blonde hair which was kept off her face with an Alice band, and she was always well dressed with smart shoes. Her mother shopped at Marks & Spencer. I looked just as smart and wore Marks & Spencer's school clothes too, but mine came from jumble sales.

Marmie couldn't afford to buy new clothes for all six of us, so on Saturday afternoons she would line up outside church halls in the posh areas to buy our school clothes. Marmie had a real flair for fashion and she used to say, "It doesn't matter what you wear, it's how you wear it and who the person is inside it." So I always wore whatever I was dressed in with pride – and often won the school prize for the best-dressed girl.

Janice and I were a pair. We made a pact to be friends for ever and that made me so happy because someone liked me for me, which is what I always wanted. She stood up for me – not that I couldn't take care of myself – and made it clear to everyone that I was her friend.

I was so thrilled when she invited me to her house for her fifteenth-birthday party along with all the other girls. None of them had ever asked me to a party before – they spoke to me at school, but never invited me to their homes. I felt so happy to be accepted completely. Marmie didn't usually let me go out with friends after school, but I persuaded her to let me go this time as the party was going to be straight after school and would be over by 7 p.m.

When we got to Janice's house, her mother smiled when she saw me – but it was not a true smile. I knew that smile and the look that came with it. It was a look that said, "What are you doing here?" Her lips smiled as though they were pulled upwards like a pair of curtains, while her eyes flicked up and down with the slightest of movements that told me my presence was not accepted. I still get that look sometimes, even today.

Janice, however, was completely oblivious to the look – she was a fun-loving, high-spirited, carefree teenager who saw only the good in everybody. Anyway, it was her birthday, and she was happy as a lark and as excited as a March hare. We all ran up to her room and got changed out of our school uniforms. I had brought with me one of my Sunday-best home-made dresses.

Some of the other girls even put on lipstick, but not me.

"Come on, try some, Floella," said Janice enthusiastically.

"No, thank you," I said, smiling. It wasn't my shade anyway, but I don't think Janice was aware of that. She just saw me as one of the girls.

We all did what fifteen-year-old girls do – giggled and had fun. Janice's mum had laid on a wonderful spread, and after the birthday cake had been cut and "Happy Birthday" sung, she said she was going out for a while and would be back before seven to see us off.

As soon as she left, there was a knock at the door and three or four boys arrived. There was now even more giggling from the girls as someone suggested we play blind man's bluff, where the boys put on blindfolds and tried to find a girl to kiss.

Well, this really worried me and made me feel a panic that sent me into a cold sweat. I wanted to be one of the girls and join in with all the fun, but this was getting serious. I was out of my depth. Marmie had put the fear of God in me when she told me her version of the facts of life when I started my periods. "You are a woman now, so that means you will get pregnant if you play around with boys, you hear me?" she'd said sternly.

"Yes, Marmie," I'd whispered in a low, embarrassed voice.

"I don't want you bringing any babies home with you ... you understand."

"Yes, Marmie," I'd said meekly. And that

had been end of my "facts-of-life education".

It had done the trick, though. I would have nothing to do with boys and made sure I was never in a situation where I had to face them. But now I had a dilemma. What was I to do? I couldn't say I didn't want to play the game, but what if someone caught me and tried to kiss me?

I had got into trouble when I first arrived in England, when I gave a boy called Norman a black eye for kissing me during a game of kiss chase in the playground, a game I hadn't understood until Norman kissed me. The other girls fancied Norman and sent me to Coventry for being the chosen one and for giving their heart-throb a black eye.

I didn't want to be handed down the same sentence again, but Marmie's words of warning rang in my ears. Suddenly I had an idea. I made a silly excuse about getting something from my bag in Janice's bedroom and hurried up the stairs. This gave me time to think. I desperately looked around the room – and then it came to me. There was only one thing to do to avoid being kissed by a dreaded boy. I flung open the wardrobe, jumped inside and slammed the door behind me. I hid there in the dark, hardly breathing, and decided to stay there until I felt it was safe to come out and go home.

I seemed to be in my refuge for ages, listening

intently for the sound of anyone coming into the room and discovering me cowering among the coats. But I don't think anyone even noticed I had disappeared – they were far too involved in the game.

Janice started to invite me to her house more regularly after school, and once or twice I went – but just for a little while, as Marmie insisted I come straight home to do my chores and my homework.

But after-school outings soon came to an abrupt end when Janice asked me to go to a local disco one evening. I really wanted to go, as I loved dancing, but when I told Marmie about it she went mad.

"No daughter of mine is going out in the evening like a *sagga* girl [a good-time girl]. You are just fifteen, and only girls with no sense of pride go gallivanting like that. Come, let me show you what I mean."

That evening she told me to get in the car, drove to the local disco and parked outside.

"Now, look at the way those girls dress to go to the disco. Look at the way the boys are hugging and kissing them. They are not treating them with any respect. You want to be treated like that?"

"No, Marmie," I cried, shaking my head vigorously.

"Right, let's go home, then, and I don't want

51

to hear any more of this going out with your friends to the disco."

The following Saturday she told me to get dressed in my best clothes – we were going dancing. She and I got on the train to Victoria, then the underground to Hammersmith, where we finally arrived at a huge, palatial ballroom. It was the Hammersmith Palais, where we danced together to the Joe Loss Big Band.

We went there often after that and we would dance the night away until 10.30 p.m. when we would make our way back home, happy and exhausted. I loved every moment of it as I was with Marmie, my protector and best friend. I felt confident – and never had any fear of getting pregnant.

Even though I didn't go to the disco with Janice, she remained my friend. I never told her Marmie didn't approve of me being friends with her, a friend who in Marmie's eyes wanted to lead me astray.

CHAPTER SEVEN

Marmie had a tight grip on the family. What she said was law. She demanded discipline and respect from us. She handed out tough love, and when she said "NO", she meant it. Dardie was the softer of the two and he left the reprimanding to Marmie. Twice I had memorable encounters with her where I ended up on the losing end.

The first one was when I was thirteen. We had all brought home our school photographs which pictured our class. My teacher had told the class she needed to know whether or not we were going to buy our photograph, and if so to bring in the money for it as soon as possible. So a few days after I'd given the photograph to Marmie, I followed my teacher's orders and said, "Are you or are you not going to pay for the photograph?" Why did I have to say those words in that tone?

"Eh, eh who do you think you are talking to, young lady?" said Marmie, with that threatening note in her voice.

I suddenly realized the full implication of what I had done, but there was no going back. "All the other girls have paid for their photograph and the teacher said, did I want mine or not," I said, trying to sound confident even though my voice was trembling.

"I have to pay for six photographs and I am not interested in what the other girls do. If you want to be like them, then go and live with them. And, to teach you a lesson for speaking to me rudely, you can take the photograph back to school. You are not having it."

"But Marmie," I pleaded.

"Don't answer me back," she snapped.

And that was the end of that. I didn't get my photograph but all my brothers and sisters got theirs. That was a hard lesson I learnt that day. Each year after that when I brought home my school photograph I patiently waited for Marmie to give me the money to pay for it in her own good time.

Another time I had a run-in with Marmie was when I questioned her about me doing all the ironing, including my brothers' shirts. "Why can't the boys iron their own shirts?" I protested.

"You have to do the ironing because you are a girl," she said, as if it were a given.

"But that's not fair!" I shouted. "Being a girl doesn't mean I should do the household chores."

Well, at that, she threw the saucepan she was holding in my direction. Fortunately I had fast reactions and ducked just in time for it to sail over my head. I quickly got down to finishing the ironing without questioning or uttering another word. But I vowed under my breath never to iron another shirt for a man when I left home, and I've kept that promise.

Marmie had always had to be tough because she'd had to fend for herself from the time she was seventeen. In 1943 she ran away from the wicked auntie she'd lived with since she was eleven, when her father died. He had brought her up alone from the age of four after her mother died.

Her mother, Winifred Charles, was from Grenada and had met my grandad William when she went to work in Trinidad. People often migrated to Trinidad, and during the time of slavery it was also the island many people fled to, in order to escape the harsher regimes on other islands. But in my grandma's time people went because Trinidad was very prosperous and work could be found in agriculture, the thriving oil industry or at Pitch Lake, which has an infinite supply of asphalt, used on roads around the world. Unlike other Caribbean islands, Trinidad only had to endure slavery for fifty years, so the harsh brutality and the deliberate practice of family separation didn't affect the people as much as on the other islands. For all these reasons Marmie's mother went to Trinidad, which was truly multicultural.

Marmie's father owned a huge cocoa plantation, in the area of Diego Martin, which had been left to him by my great-grandfather, a freed enslaved man from Tobago named King David Drice. He was married to a Scottish woman named Fitz Drice, who wore her hair in long plaits wrapped around the crown of her head. As a child Marmie saw a photograph of her and she told us Grandma Fitz was stunningly beautiful. Together the two of them had nine children, my grandfather William Drice being one of the eldest.

In my great-grandfather's will, it was decreed that Great Grandma Fitz was entitled to an allowance of five shillings (25p) as long as she never remarried and lived a moral life. She never did remarry, as she was devoted to my great-grandfather.

I have always wondered where in Scotland she was from and what my Scottish ancestors were like. It was not unusual to find Scottish or Irish people living in the Caribbean and marrying African freed enslaved partners, as many of them were banished or deported themselves to the Caribbean by the British Government, sometimes because of their religious or political beliefs, sometimes simply for stealing a loaf of bread. The first people to be taken to Barbados by the English to work the land were the Irish, then the Scots, before millions of Africans were finally brought in as enslaved people to work the sugar plantations.

This was the beginning of the cruel and

terrible period of the slave trade, which lasted over two hundred years. The plantations and the slave trade became a source of great wealth and importance to Britain, Spain, France, Portugal, Holland and, to a lesser extent, Sweden and Denmark. Many great European cities were built on the vast profits made from sugar and African blood.

There still remains a strong European influence in the Caribbean. In Jamaica, there is a community of Germans living in a place called Seaford Town, where they settled nearly two hundred years ago. In Montserrat there is a strong Irish influence, so much so that the island is known as the Emerald Isle. The inhabitants even celebrate St Patrick's Day – the only other place, other than Ireland and the USA, to do so. The tradition there is to stamp a shamrock in visitors' passports when they arrive to show the island's Irish heritage.

My great-grandfather was a very respected landowner in his community, and my grandfather continued the tradition of producing the finest cocoa in the area. Trinidad is known for cultivating the best-quality cocoa; in fact its cocoa is exported around the world, and the most expensive chocolate sold is more than likely to contain Trinidadian cocoa.

When my grandfather died, the land was snatched by his siblings, and my mother was excluded from gaining any benefit from the plantation or the land. She had to work her way up from possessing very little, struggling to make ends meet – but always with her dignity and pride in place.

She believed that the harder you worked, the luckier you became. She worked hard for the people she was sent to live with after her father died. They were her father's relatives and were very affluent people. They even had a telephone (very unusual in those days), because my great-aunt was a midwife and had to be constantly on call in any emergency.

But Marmie was treated like a servant, the Cinderella of the family, constantly at their beck and call. She was not even allowed to go to school. They felt she was only fit to clean up after them. She polished their grand piano and wooden floors and vowed her children would never end up doing the same for others. Eventually she could take no more and, after several failed attempts, ran away for good.

I think all that cleaning had a long-term effect on Marmie: it made her very house proud and she loved to see a clean, shiny house. Sandra and I had to do our fair share of polishing as part of our daily home chores, and to while away the time as we worked we would sing the blues. That was when Marmie didn't have her Jim Reeves records playing. Jim Reeves was an American country singer; she loved his songs and would sing along in her what could only be described as unmelodic tones.

One of my other chores was doing the weekly washing and I hated it. I would have to fill the bathtub with water to soak the endless amount of laundry generated by all eight members of the family. We didn't have a washing machine so I had to use a washboard, which was an old-fashioned device for washing clothes. It was a piece of wood with about ten raised rows on which I had to rub the dirty clothes back and forth. There was no washing powder; instead I would have to smear a piece of bright red carbolic soap over the garments, then rub them vigorously up and down the washboard. This gave me huge blisters on my hands, but it was something that had to be done and I was the designated washerwoman. I detested this chore so much that, at the age of fifteen when I got a Saturday job in Woolworth's for which I was paid the huge sum of eighteen shillings, I gave fifteen to Marmie, to put towards the cost of buying a washing machine – a Hotpoint twin tub. I rejoiced the day the machine was delivered and plumbed in. It meant I would never have to bend over scrubbing a tubful of dirty clothes again. Seven years later, Marmie gave the same twin tub back to me when I moved into my own flat.

CHAPTER EIGHT

My last two years at school were eventful and exciting ones. I was never happier to be there, as I no longer felt like an outsider and no longer saw my colour as an obstacle, even though it confronted others with their prejudices. I loved my brown skin despite the fact that it might hold me back from reaching my full potential. I was content to accept whatever opportunities came my way and was prepared to take the long journey that lay ahead. My only responsibility was to make sure I made the most of any given opportunity, by playing my part in a positive way and never wishing to be someone else.

One thing that helped me play my part with great satisfaction was being at school with a visionary headmistress, who made it easy for me to experience life in a fulfilling way.

She was Miss Bowles, whose enormous bust seemed to arrive in the room before she did. She had a mischievous twinkle in her eye and a mysterious Mona Lisa smile, which told you she had a plan that she would make happen come what may. She wanted the best for her girls and we had to behave like proper well-brought-up young ladies. I only got told off by her once – and it was not really my fault I got into her bad books.

It happened because I was protecting a girl who was being bullied because she was skinny.

She was so thin that you felt if the wind blew strongly enough she would blow away. I saw some boys picking on her as I walked home. I knew what it was like to be picked on for no good reason. So, instead of minding my own business, I got in between them and challenged the boys. "Leave her alone, you big bullies," I screamed, ready to take them on.

"You gonna make us?" sneered one of them.

"Yes," I said, shielding the poor defenceless girl who stood trembling, frightened as a little mouse.

Just then, who should come driving by but Miss Bowles, who simply called out, "You girl! Stop that brawling in the street and get home right now," before driving off.

The next morning during assembly there was no twinkle in her eye or smile on her face as she announced in a steely voice, "I want the girl who brought shame on the Penge Girls' School uniform yesterday afternoon to come forward."

There was a hush in the large hall. Everyone looked straight ahead as Miss Bowles waited patiently for the culprit to step forward. Being one of the handful of Caribbean girls in the school I was easily visible and readily picked out in a crowd. There was no hiding-place for me, so I took a deep breath and stepped forward.

The deafening silence was interrupted by gasps from the other girls as I passed.

61

Somehow I got to the front of the stage, where Miss Bowles stood to attention like a sergeant major. "Turn and face the whole school," she commanded, "and tell them your name."

Slowly, I turned. "My name is Floella Benjamin," I said sheepishly.

"Floella Benjamin, you were seen behaving in an unladylike manner in the street in your school uniform. This has brought shame and disgrace upon the school. Please apologize to the school for doing so."

I bravely made an attempt to explain what had happened and why she had seen me in that situation. "I was just—"

"We are waiting for your apology," she interrupted.

I realized she was in no mood to listen, but I stuttered on. "I was only trying to help—"

"We don't want to hear your excuses; there is no excuse for your despicable behaviour."

So I reluctantly said, "Please forgive me, everyone."

"Now go and stand outside my door for all to see and remain there for the rest of the day."

I walked out of the assembly feeling the sentence was so unfair. I had taken on the skinny girl's battle – yet she hadn't stood up for me when I needed her.

Despite this encounter, Miss Bowles proved to be a fair head for she never held the incident against me. Once I had served my punishment, the slate was wiped clean. She even selected me to be a prefect later on, and I did my best to uphold the high standards she insisted upon from her girls.

She in turn provided many unusual opportunities that girls attending a secondary modern school would never otherwise have had. As well as insisting we all have good manners, she believed we should never be overawed by any social circumstances we found ourselves in. So she invited the legendary Peggy Spencer to the school to teach us proper ballroom dancing.

Peggy Spencer was a famous dance teacher with a championship-winning ballroom dance group who competed all over the world. We learnt how to waltz, jive and cha-cha-cha. We even had our very own formation-dance team. Miss Bowles always took great delight in watching us sweep across the floor with our heads held high. Her smile was infectious.

However, I do remember that smile not being part of her presence when Winston Churchill died in 1965.

She arranged for a television set to be brought into the school hall, and announced in a solemn voice, "Girls, one of the great men of our times has died. He served our country beyond the call of duty during the Second World War and it's because of him that you children are free to live as you do." As I stared at the television screen in silence, I thought about the heroic stories Dardie had told us of the many thousands of Caribbean men and women who had fought in both the First and the Second World Wars, also to secure our freedom. In fact, Dardie's own brother had died fighting in the Second World War, like many other Caribbeans who had answered the call to fight and protect the Empire, King and country. I remember Dardie saying that he wished their contribution was remembered here in Britain the same as that of everyone else who fought in the war.

There was only one other leader's death, two years earlier, that had affected our lives in a similar way to that of Churchill. It was the death of John F. Kennedy, the President of the United States of America, who was assassinated in the back of his car as he was being driven along in Dallas, Texas. Marmie and Dardie always said Kennedy seemed to have empathy with the struggle our race faced daily like no other leader at the time.

I remember that historic moment when his life was snuffed out quite clearly. Sandra and I were washing the dishes in the kitchen, my other brothers and sister were happily playing, and Dardie was away on one of his music trips. Marmie was busy at her sewing machine in the front room. The television, which had a piece of multi-coloured, shaded plastic stuck on the front to make it look as though the black and white picture was in colour, was on.

Suddenly we heard Marmie give a loud scream and she started to cry out repeatedly, "They've killed a great man, they've killed a great man!" We all rushed to see what was going on, what was causing her to be so distraught. On the screen was a confused scene of people standing in shock and amazement. The announcer solemnly said, "The President is dead." And Marmie wailed even louder.

A few years later, in 1968, another prospect of hope and equality was taken from us. Martin Luther King, the voice of peaceful change, was assassinated. We wept for days and there was a depressing feeling of gloom and sadness in our house. He had been a great inspiration to us because of his words of wisdom and Dardie used to recite his "freedom march" speech to us – he knew it off by heart. He even put in his will that he wanted the speech played at his funeral and in 2007 we granted his wish.

Martin Luther King had predicted that one day a man of colour would preside in the White House. It seemed an impossible dream at that time, and the vision of hope was snuffed out of our lives when he was murdered. Little did we realize that his prophecy would be fulfilled – in 2008, when Barack Obama was elected the first black President of America. Obama's charismatic personality has become a symbol of hope to the world and changed millions of people's thinking by breaking down barriers. I wept openly the night he was elected, and wished Marmie and Dardie had lived to see that historic moment.

But forty-three years earlier, it was the death of Winston Churchill that brought an outpouring of grief from the British nation. We sat and watched respectfully, only the funereal music under the sombre voice of Richard Dimbleby cutting through the silence in the hall as we stared at what was taking place at Westminster Abbey. The emotion was too much for some of the girls, who cried as we watched the thousands of people gathered at the Abbey to pay their final respects to the great leader, his coffin draped in the Union Jack.

Churchill had become the nation's hero after the victorious end of the Second World War in 1945. Years later, when he lost the election and was defeated as Prime Minister, he felt he had lost touch with the British people. Little did he realize that they still held him so close to their hearts. Some of the girls didn't fully understand the importance of his leadership, but we knew we had to follow Miss Bowles and show respect.

I looked up briefly from the flickering black and white screen and saw the tears rolling down her cheeks. She took out the folded white cotton handkerchief that she always had tucked into the waist of her navy blue skirt, under her large bosoms, and wiped away the tears. There was definitely no smile on her face that day.

CHAPTER NINE

The sound of music could always be heard in our house in one form or another. When Dardie was home, he would either be practising on his tenor saxophone or listening to his jazz records on the huge Blue Spot radiogram, which played his precious, breakable, shiny black liquorice-like discs at various speeds: the smallest discs at 45 revolutions per minute, the old-fashioned middle-size ones at 78, and the larger modern long-playing ones at $33\frac{1}{3}$ rpm.

The records were lovingly dusted and treasured, for if a speck of dust touched the delicate needle as it danced around the spinning disc, a shrieking noise would be heard interrupting the melodic sound coming from the speakers. There were other makes of radiogram, but for us Caribbeans the Blue Spot was the one to have, as it had the best sound. This classic piece of 1950s furniture was the centrepiece of our front room; it was something all West Indian families saved up to buy and cherished. When it was not being used, the lid was closed and a stiffly starched, crocheted doily would sit on the top with a vase of plastic flowers placed in the middle.

I suppose the radiogram was essential to our well-being, as it kept part of our culture alive and the music reminded us of our homeland back in the Caribbean. Many people had brought their records with them when they came here, as in those days it was difficult to buy Caribbean records in England. So we also listened to popular singers of the fifties and sixtees like Nat King Cole, Ray Charles, Lonnie Donegan, Dickie Valentine and Jim Reeves, until gradually Caribbean music such as ska and reggae started to catch on and become popular even with English people.

Interestingly – and to my surprise – it was only when I came to Britain that I realized each Caribbean island had its own particular kind of music. In Trinidad, it was calypso and steel pan which Dardie used to play when we lived there (he always wanted to play jazz, too – his first love – which was rarely played over there). The Jamaican music at that time was ska and rock steady; reggae came later, partly through the music of the legendary and brilliant Bob Marley. His poetic and philosophical words addressing every emotion imaginable, all set to the reggae beat, were infectious. I never heard this type of music until I came to Britain and I loved it. Dardie bought a few of the Jamaican records, and whenever we had visitors Marmie would make me do the latest dance for our guests. Dancing to rock steady was brilliant. It left me feeling quite exhilarated as I stepped up on my toes and shook my legs vigorously to the beat, trying to keep my balance as I did so.

When Dardie practised his saxophone we all had to keep quiet as he emulated the tones of the two great saxophonists Sonny Rollins and John Coltrane. He played with several dance bands as well as groups with which he toured for months at a time. To find work in a band he would go to Archer Street, behind Shaftesbury Avenue in London's West End, where all the jazz musicians congregated and exchanged information about bands that needed new members.

Once, when he couldn't find work in a jazz band, he joined a rhythm 'n' blues band called the Mohicans and had to dress like a Mohican Indian with face paint, feathered headdress and white suede, fringed outfit. The band was very popular and quite unique so was always top of the bill. They had pop groups like the Rolling Stones as their support act. But, almost overnight, the pop groups became so popular that the kind of music Dardie played was not wanted any more and he found himself out of work.

He was furious and hated this new type of music that was hitting the airwaves, so we were forbidden to listen to it at home. That's why groups like the Beatles were not part of my teenage culture. Mind you, I did have a picture of Elvis, which I got free in *Jackie* magazine, but I kept it hidden in my school general-studies book, out of sight from Dardie.

It was a difficult time for Dardie, and in

order to get work he started to travel abroad more often. His trip to Liberia, in Africa, was one that would have a long-lasting effect on my life. He sent a postcard to us with a picture of a beautiful African woman on it. She was dressed in traditional African clothes and her hair was plaited. Each plait was decorated with bright red beads.

I looked at the picture adoringly. I wanted to look like that. I felt a strong pull towards my African roots and a great desire to celebrate them and find out more about who I was and where I came from. I knew that one day I would plait my hair like that African beauty – but not while I was at school.

Marmie was starting to feel the pressure of looking after us alone, especially when Dardie travelled abroad. One night we overheard her in their bedroom telling him forcefully, "Roy, I've had enough. I can't take the pressure of looking after these six children on my own any longer. I want you to start spending more time here in England."

"But you know there's no jobs for my kind of music here in England," protested Dardie.

"Well, you will just have to find a steady job that brings in regular money."

"I'm not going to give up my music."

"Then you can form a band here and play on weekends," she said, coming up with a solution

71

she had obviously given much thought to.

Taken aback by her logic, Dardie was finally persuaded. So he set about forming his own band, with fellow Caribbean musicians who had also found themselves out of work. They played mostly in pubs and working men's clubs and at weddings, which served to satisfy his musical needs.

Once the band got booked to play at an Irish pub on St Patrick's Day. When they turned up the landlord asked Dardie, "Do you play Irish music?"

"No!" said Dardie. "We play jazz."

"Well if I were you I would make a run for it before the customers hear you," retorted the landlord.

And with that Dardie and his combo left swiftly without payment!

One day Dardie announced he wanted a girl singer for the band and, because the money he was paid for gigs was very low, he thought he would keep most of it in the family. So he got Sandra and me to audition.

Now, we sang around the house while we did the housework and I, of course, sang in the school choir and at the school concert. But to go on stage and sing publicly was quite a different matter. But Dardie insisted we had to sing for him and we were given a song to learn.

"Sandra and Floella, I want you to learn this

song. It's called 'The Lady Is a Tramp'."

"Yes, Dardie," we said, smiling nervously at each other.

"When you are ready you can both come and perform it while I play along on the saxophone."

We had heard the song being sung by Ella Fitzgerald time and time again on the Blue Spot radiogram, so it didn't take long for us to learn it. Sandra, being the elder, had to sing first. She had a lovely soprano voice which complemented my deeper tones – but this time we couldn't sing together, we had to sing alone.

"Come on, Sandra, let me hear you. After three..."

She stepped forward in front of Dardie. He played the intro and gave her the cue to come in – but she missed it.

"Come on, Sandra, don't be nervous," he said reassuringly.

Sandra looked nervously over at me, but I couldn't help her.

He played the intro once again and this time she came in on time. But her sweet voice trembled with fright and got quieter and quieter as her shyness got the better of her, until she finally gave up.

Then it was my turn. "Come on, Floella," said Dardie in a schoolmaster-type voice, "let me see what *you* can do with the song."

I pictured Ella Fitzgerald singing the song

and tried to imagine I was her on stage with the Duke Ellington band. Dardie had partly named me after her, so now it was my turn to see if I could pretend to be her. (He had given most of his children the names of jazz musicians: Lester after Lester Young, Ellington after Duke Ellington, and me after Ella Fitzgerald.)

He played the intro again and I started to click my fingers to the beat. I burst into song, feeling as though I was singing in front of a crowd and enjoying every moment of it. I was not shy and played the part of a singer. When the song ended, everyone in the family applauded and Sandra rushed over and hugged me; perhaps she was relieved that she didn't have to sing with the band.

"You're quite a showgirl," said Dardie proudly. "I think you can make it as a singer in the band."

He gave me some more songs to learn, and I practised with him and listened to singers like Sarah Vaughan and Lena Horne, until he felt I was ready for my first gig.

"We have a booking for a wedding," he announced, "and you will be singing with the band, Floella."

I was really excited and rushed to get Marmie's advice on what to wear.

The wedding was at Anerley Town Hall, an old Victorian grey-stone building with a grand entrance framed by ornate Grecian-style pillars. Beyond the carpeted entrance was an enormous function room with large chandeliers above a polished wooden dance floor. At the far end of the room was a stage where Dardie had set up for the gig, which was a West Indian wedding.

Now West Indian weddings can only be described as "spectacular". The bride would always be dressed in traditional white, with numerous layers of petticoats under a voluminous skirt. Brilliant white gloves were obligatory, and were only taken off for the band of gold to be lovingly placed on her finger. Her hair would be decorated with flowers and pearls, then covered in a delicate white lace veil. Her bridesmaids would be similarly decked out, usually in pink, blue, lilac or yellow. The groom would be equally flamboyant, in a suit fit for a movie star, tailor-made, double-breasted and complete with a carnation or rose in the buttonhole. His outfit would be matched by those of his best man and close friends.

The guests, young and old, would also be dressed up to the nines in their colourful and most stylish clothes. Yes, a wedding was the time to dress up in all your finery and enjoy every moment of the occasion.

The buffet tables would be creaking under the weight of huge bowls of curry, rotis, rice, stewed chicken and, of course, the multilayered, dark, rich Caribbean wedding cake, bursting with rum trying to get through the white icing decorated with pretty iced flowers.

The music was an important part of the celebrations, so when Dardie and his band struck up on the stage at Anerley Town Hall, everyone got to their feet to show off the latest dance movements. When my cue came to stand in front of the microphone and sing, I took a deep breath, opened my mouth and sang out to my heart's content. It was show time, and I had a ball – for while I was singing, I felt as if I was soaring through space to another planet and I loved the journey there and back.

A few years later it was Lester and Ellington's turn to audition for a place in the band. With this in mind, Dardie had insisted that they learn to play a musical instrument. He decided Lester should play the drums and Ellington should take up the piano, like his namesake Duke Ellington.

They were both pretty good musicians and got special coaching from Dardie on how to play jazz with feeling. He would stamp his feet hard and say, "Listen to the beat and keep time!" Sometimes he would get overexcited when we were in full swing, partly owing to the amount of alcohol he drank – like most jazz musicians he loved to have a drink.

Marmie was delegated as our driver when

we went to gigs. She didn't have a musical ear (although she would sometimes take a turn on the maracas so as not to get bored while she waited for us), but she was great at organizing and planning our routes to the various gigs in and around London over the four years we played together. We even played once at Wormwood Scrubs prison and at the magnificent Chelsea Town Hall.

We would pack all the instruments carefully into our large Ford Zephyr, with the drum kit securely strapped to the roof rack, and off we would go in all types of weather, never quite sure what to expect or what sort of reception we would get when we played. One thing that surprised me, though, was that we never had to face any racial abuse or discrimination. Music seemed to transcend all barriers, and musicians were not judged on their colour but on their ability to entertain. We made a great sound as we meticulously followed Dardie's instructions and kept the beat. We were a tight band – it was a real family affair. I was never inhibited when it came to performing, and stage fright was not something I ever felt.

Dardie always used to tell me the story of how when I was fifteen months old, in Trinidad, he had taken Sandra and me to a Boxing Day party at which he was playing. He had taken us along because Marmie was due to give birth (to my brother Lester), so she wanted us out of the house. Apparently I got onto the stage, announced to the audience that they weren't dancing properly, and proceeded to show them how to dance to the music.

I never intended to become a performer – my love was teaching and I longed to become a teacher; that was my dream. But what I didn't realize then was that the years spent performing with Dardie, Lester and Ellington would stand me in good stead for my future career.

A life in the limelight at that time was not even an option. Marmie wanted me to have a profession, a "proper job". A career in music and show business was certainly not that. She told us time and time again that she had made sacrifices to bring us to England so that we could get a good education and go on to make a difference to society by getting a professional job. So the idea of any of us following in Dardie's footsteps, by pursuing a career in show business, which never brought in regular money, was not something she wanted for her children. Music as a hobby was fine, but was certainly not seen as a career for any of her precious children.

Mind you, when we misbehaved and she found us too much to cope with, Marmie used to say, "If I had my life to live over, I would only have half of you." And in chorus we would all say, "Which half?"

CHAPTER TEN

After Sandra had come almost bottom of the class, Marmie gave up going to work at the laundry and was at home with us in the evenings, making sure we all did our homework properly. She also insisted we all go to the library to do extra studying. Sandra loved reading and would spend hours with her head in a book, devouring every scrap of information. Like Dardie she had a brain like an encyclopaedia, full of knowledge. I was never too keen on reading but loved maths, geography, history and science. I adored subjects that helped me discover and learn more about the world.

I loved French, too, partly because of my French teacher, who only spoke to us in French whenever she saw us anywhere around the school. The sound of her beautiful French accent just made me want to learn. I would try to repeat what she said, parrot-fashion. The first phrase I learnt was "ouvre la fenêtre". I still remember it so well. I would pout my lips, my tongue would caress the words and I would try to imitate being French. But unfortunately, the more we progressed in the lessons the harder I found it. The construction of the verbs always got me and I could read French more easily than I could speak it. I did get a prize for French on Speech Day, though, not because I was brilliant, no – it was "E" for effort.

My French teacher was lovely and kind in the generosity she showed to her pupils. There is nothing better to make you feel good about yourself than when a teacher gives you encouragement. You remember it for ever and a good relationship shared during those precious school years is everlasting. Unfortunately, so is a bad relationship, the sort you have with unsympathetic teachers who show little or no confidence in their pupils but see them as enemies, not as little treasures. I had several of these to contend with during my schooldays. I wonder if those teachers ever realized how much they could break children's hearts and scar them for life.

I knew if I ever had the privilege of becoming a teacher, I would see it as a chance to touch future leaders and to hand over the gift of education lovingly to each pupil. I would aspire to motivate children, the way my French teacher motivated me.

As much as Marmie wanted us to have professional careers, the reality of our financial situation didn't make it easy. There were six of us to keep at school and very little money coming in for our upkeep. So when Sandra was sixteen she had to leave to help with the finances. Staying on at school to do her A levels and then going to university was not an option.

But Marmie still had her sights set on us

getting a good job when we left school. So an appointment was made to see the careers officer who came to meet the school leavers and their parents.

Sandra's and Marmie's appointment to see Mrs Barratt was to be a life-changing experience for all three of them. Sandra had set her heart on working for a pharmaceutical company called Wellcome Research Laboratory, which was not far from where we lived. It was in Beckenham, in Kent, a very middle-class Conservative area.

Mrs Barratt was a large woman in her fifties. She always wore a white blouse, a grey skirt and a small black felt hat perched on her head at a slightly jaunty angle. She was the sort of woman who would always wear gloves if she was going out, white ones in the summer.

Sandra and Marmie sat across the table from her and she smiled at them politely. "Well, Sandra, what type of job would you like to do?" said Mrs Barratt in a rather condescending way.

"I would like to be a research technician at Wellcome," said Sandra in her quiet voice.

"Oh, I'm terribly sorry, Sandra," said Mrs Barratt, rather taken aback at my sister's answer. "I'm afraid they don't take coloured people there. I can find you a job as a nursery nurse, but it's impossible for me to recommend you for a job at Wellcome."

These words were like a red rag to a bull as far as Marmie was concerned. "What exactly do you mean by that?" she interrupted. "I have made sure my children are well educated, and they have studied hard with the intention of having professional careers, and you are sitting there and telling me my daughter can't get a job where she wants to because of the colour of her skin, even though she has the ability."

"Yes, I'm sorry, Mrs Benjamin, that is correct. But I am happy to find her work where coloured people are accepted – although it won't be in a prestigious position."

"My children will find work wherever they set their minds on and no one will stop them or stand in their way," said Marmie with an air of determination. "I will prove that to you."

"I'm sorry you feel like that, Mrs Benjamin, but that is the way it is," said Mrs Barratt, with a note of finality in her voice.

When Marmie and Sandra arrived home, Marmie was still furious and Sandra was sobbing her heart out. We all looked on, wondering if it was going to be the same for the rest of us, and whether it was worth bothering to study as hard as we did if we were never going to be accepted for a good job when we tried to get one.

At that time people from the Caribbean were expected to do the menial jobs in factories, or to be bus conductors or cleaners. They were, however, also accepted as nurses: many young Caribbean women were asked to come to Britain to work in hospitals as there was a shortage of nurses after the war. Thousands of young women took up the call to come and train to be nurses in hospitals all over the country, in cities, towns and even small villages. Many of them had to put up with prejudice not just from the patients they cared for but even more so from their colleagues. Nevertheless, they bravely persevered and fulfilled their duties, becoming fully trained and dedicated nurses.

Shamefully, over the following years, hardly any of them ever got promoted to matron. The glass ceiling was firmly in place and they were not expected to break through the toughened glass.

Marmie was a fighter, though; remember, she had been fighting for survival for nearly three decades, ever since she was eleven. She had vowed her children would be successful, and she believed that all the adversities she had personally endured were for a reason. So, with that fighting spirit in full flow, like a boxer ready to take on her opponent for the championship title, she called Sandra. "Stop that crying, Sandra," she commanded. "We're going to show that Mrs Barratt. Get some paper and a pen and write an application to Wellcome. You are brilliant at

English – tell them about yourself and why you want to work for them."

Sandra diligently sat down to writing the application as commanded by Marmie and the letter was sent off immediately.

To our delight, a week later a letter arrived from Wellcome and even though it was addressed to Sandra, Marmie opened it. None of us had ever had a letter addressed to us before, but one for Sandra was expected: it must be the one we had all been anxiously waiting for.

Marmie tore open the envelope eagerly and smiled. "Read it, Sandra," she said triumphantly.

Sandra took the letter in her trembling hands and began to read to herself.

"Read the letter out loud, so everyone can hear," Marmie insisted.

"'Dear Sandra Benjamin, you have been selected to attend the first round of interviews which will take place in two weeks' time. Please let us know if you are able to attend.'"

We all jumped for joy. Marmie had won the first round.

Sandra was not very good at combing her hair in a stylish way – I had always combed it for her even when we were little. So on the day of the interview I busied myself styling her hair just right. Marmie had made her a special three-piece suit:

a stylish mustard-coloured skirt and jacket, with a flowery blouse to go underneath. When Sandra put it on she looked like a professional, oozing authority.

"Don't forget to hold your head up high when you get there," said Marmie. "Don't show them you are shy; walk with confidence and look them in the eye."

Of course Marmie was going to take Sandra to the interview – she wasn't going to leave anything to chance. So off they went and we waved goodbye. "Good luck, Sandra," we all shouted.

When they reached Wellcome they found the layout of the site quite confusing. The laboratory was spread over several acres and it wasn't clear what the many buildings on the site were for. I suppose it was that way for security reasons because the laboratory researched new clinical drugs.

Marmie and Sandra wandered around helplessly, until they saw a man in a dark suit going into a building carrying a file. Before he could enter, Marmie said, "Excuse me, we've come for an interview..."

"Try that building over there," said the man dismissively as he hurriedly went inside.

When they got there, they found he had directed them to the building where interviews for cleaners and bottle-washers were being held. Finally they were redirected back to the building where they had asked the man for directions. They went in and sat with the other anxious applicants, until it was their turn to go into the interview room.

To their surprise, the interview was being conducted by the same man in the dark suit. He too looked astonished to see Marmie and Sandra again – clearly he had assumed they were going to the interviews for cleaning jobs. But after he got over his initial embarrassment, he began asking Sandra questions about herself.

When Marmie started to answer on Sandra's behalf, she was politely told, "Mrs Benjamin, it is Sandra's views I want to hear, so will you please let her answer the questions."

Marmie found it hard to stay quiet as she was worried Sandra would let her shyness get the better of her. But somehow Sandra controlled her nerves and answered all the questions intelligently, telling the interviewer about her journey to England and how she had got to where she was. He listened with interest as she spoke of her aspirations eloquently and with confidence. She wasn't going to let herself miss this golden opportunity to fulfil her dream.

"Well, thank you for coming, Sandra," he said. "I have fifty applicants to interview and after I have seen them all I will write to you one way or the other."

We waited weeks for the letter to arrive; it

was excruciating. After a while, Sandra began to lose heart. "Mrs Barratt was right when she said they don't take coloured people at Wellcome," she exclaimed, resigning herself to failure and rejection.

"No news is good news," replied Marmie in her ever confident way. "Just be patient."

Time seemed to drag on and it was hard to concentrate on our school work. The outcome of this saga would affect the future of all six of us. Marmie believed she could win the battle we faced daily to be accepted in a hostile society, where because of our colour the extent of our capabilities was decided before we had a chance to show our ability. This injustice was going to be even more difficult to cope with in the adult world as we tried to forge a career. There was a certain sadness in the house. Sandra and I sang the blues more than ever as we tried to busy ourselves.

Then, out of the darkness that had engulfed us, came the flicker of light that was going to show us which path the next stage of our journey would take. It was the letter from Wellcome.

This time, Marmie said, "Sandra, you open it and read out what it says."

Sandra was trembling more than ever as she clumsily tried to open the envelope. We all held our breath. I shut my eyes and waited for the words of the letter to fill the room. But no sound came from Sandra; she just stared into space.

"What does it say?" I shouted.

"Yes, tell us!" everyone yelled.

"Give it to me," said Marmie.

But before she could read it, Sandra found her voice and cried with delight, "I've got the job – they want me, they want me!"

The noise we all made was like a crowd at a football match when their team scores. We shouted, danced and screamed with joy and happiness.

Marmie had won the fight. She had believed that nothing could stop her and her children. All we had to do was work hard and reach for the sky. She had shown us anything was possible.

Sandra went on to work for Wellcome for over thirty years and her confidence grew more and more. She made a very successful career for herself, ending up as Senior Training Manager for the company and, like Dardie and Grandad Leonard, promoted equality and diversity.

At the end of that school year, by a strange coincidence, Marmie found herself sitting next to Mrs Barratt at Speech Day. She leaned over and said in a very loud voice, "Mrs Barratt, Sandra got a job at Wellcome, you know – the one you said she wouldn't get. She's been accepted!"

Mrs Barratt blushed with embarrassment and adjusted her black hat nervously. Marmie had definitely won the final round. After that, she and Mrs Barratt formed a wonderful relationship and worked together to make sure all six of us got the best opportunities to secure our futures.

CHAPTER ELEVEN

Like Sandra, I had to leave school at sixteen to go to work and help take away some of the financial burden on Marmie and Dardie. I really didn't want to leave school – I loved being exposed to knowledge and adored practising the art of learning and making sense of what I was being taught. I wasn't very good at theory; I was a more practical, creative learner. I would use my imagination and visualize what was being shared with me by my teachers, with Marmie's mantra ringing in my ears: "Education is your passport to life."

For my white friends, spending every minute of their day learning was not important. Constant studying was not as high on their list of priorities. "Have fun and do just enough to get by" was their philosophy. But that was not the Caribbean way. "Work, work, work; study hard to improve your life" is what we were told relentlessly.

Our philosophy drove me on like a racehorse, galloping along at full speed. Sometimes I did slip into the white culture at school – I had to; it was a way of fitting in. Living in two cultures came easy: Caribbean at home with a strict regime and then morphing into a less restrictive existence at school. I felt like a chameleon. My friend Janice encouraged me to be like her, but I could only do so at school. I would never get away with it at home, especially in front of Marmie.

The pact Janice and I had made to always be friends was still in place and we often talked about staying together for ever. We even planned to work at the same place when we left school. We vowed to be inseparable.

So having to leave school was made more bearable, because I felt that at least Janice and I would still see each other after we'd left. All the other girls were excited about leaving. One girl in particular had good reason to be excited because she could then tell the world she was going out with the school gardener. She was a tall, long-legged blonde who wore her school uniform as though she were a model. She looked far beyond her sixteen years in the way she walked and talked. She always hitched her skirt up so that it was above her knees, and her blouse looked as though it was two sizes too small for her as it struggled to cover her well-developed breasts. She was the envy of us all, as the boys were drawn to her like bees to a honey pot.

She would tell us unbelievable stories of what happened when she went out with them. The details of her kissing with tongues and "petting sessions" fascinated me. I was sweet sixteen and never been kissed – well, apart from when Norman kissed me when I was ten, and I punched him for doing so.

I did want someone to kiss me, but was far too afraid to let that happen: Marmie had told me that I must have nothing to do with boys or I would end up a teenage mother. As I couldn't kiss anyone for real, I used to dream of doing so one day. To make sure I would know what to do, I would practise in secret for when the moment arrived.

I would go to the bedroom I shared with my sisters, make sure no one was around and close the door. Then I would open our large mahogany wardrobe and look towards the small mirror on the inside of the door. I would move intimately forward as though the mirror was a handsome boy, close my eyes and press my lips against the cold smooth glass, moving them passionately, trying to get as much realism as I could. Eventually I would breathe out with a sigh as I opened my eyes – only to find the mirror steamed up from the condensation of my hot breath. I would wipe away the mist and smile to myself. I knew one day when I had a real pair of lips to kiss I would be ready – my practising would not be in vain.

For us girls that final year at school was the beginning of adulthood. By now we had all celebrated our sixteenth birthdays. I still hadn't had a party and I never got any presents on my special day. But Marmie always baked a cake on each of our birthdays – she thought food and love were the best gifts any child could receive. I remember I wished I could have a special party and presents like Janice, whose parents gave her Marks & Spencer shares for her sixteenth birthday. She told me her mum had said they were a legacy for the future. It was only much later that I realized that the legacy Marmie had given me was far more valuable.

The legacy Mrs Bowles wanted for us was to be proud of our time at school and to leave as well-brought-up young ladies. Preparing for the outside world was hard, and that year we all studied diligently for our GCEs (which are now called GCSEs). We also had the obligatory meeting with Mrs Barratt to decide on our careers.

This time Mrs Barratt had an air of admiration when she met Marmie. "Hello, Mrs Benjamin, it's good to meet you again. And what career is Floella interested in?"

"Hello, Mrs Barratt," said Marmie with a winning smile. "Floella would like to be a teacher, but unfortunately my husband and I can't afford to keep her on at school to take her A levels."

"That's a shame," said Mrs Barratt sympathetically.

"Oh, but she will be going to night classes to

take the exams, and then go on to teacher training college," announced Marmie confidently. "She's good at figures, so in the meantime, to earn some money, she'd like to work in a bank."

I thought this was a great idea because my friend Janice wanted to work in a bank too, and she said we should work at the same place. "Do you have any idea which bank you would like to work for, Floella?" Mrs Barratt asked earnestly.

"I would like to work for Barclays Bank," I said eagerly, which was what Janice had told me to say.

"Leave it to me and I will arrange an interview at Barclays for you, as well as a few other banks, just in case."

A few weeks later Marmie took me to the interview at Barclays headquarters in the City. I had to go in alone to be interviewed and she had to remain outside. For the first time in my life I felt nervous, even though I knew I had all the necessary qualifications. This was an important episode in my life; I had to make an impression and get the job if Janice and I were to work at the same place.

As I sat across the huge desk from the woman interviewer, who was dressed in a navy-blue suit with a crisp white blouse, my stomach started to churn. My knee began to shake uncontrollably, knocking against the desk so hard it almost lifted it into the air like a bouncing ball. The loud thumping noise filled the room and the woman looked up at me as she tried to write down my answer to a question she had just asked. But, even though she stared at me, I couldn't control my knee – it just kept shaking! I simply smiled at her, and she smiled back sympathetically.

I'm sure she took pity on me, and I certainly made an impression on her – although not exactly in the way I had intended – because a few weeks later I got a letter telling me I had a job at Barclays if I wanted it. I had also gone for three other interviews, where I was my confident self and not at all nervous, and they too were successful. But the job at Barclays was the one I wanted, because it meant my best friend and I would be together.

Janice had got the same acceptance letter a few days before me and I couldn't wait to tell her my good news. But my excitement was suddenly quashed by the devastating, unexpected news *she* gave *me*: "I have decided to go and work for another bank," she said in a cold, matter-of-fact way. "My mother thinks it's best. I'd better be off – see you later."

I watched her go, shocked, in disbelief at her bombshell. The feeling of rejection left me standing there like a lost soul wanting to be taken in. My heart felt as though someone had pierced it with an ice pick. Slowly the realization of what my so-called friend had told me seeped into my numb brain. My mouth went dry and my tongue felt heavy, paralysed. I couldn't call out to her and beg her to change her mind. I felt betrayed – my loyalty to her was not reciprocated. The pact we had made for what I thought would be our lasting friendship had, at that moment, come to a juddering end. My joy and excitement fizzled away, like a sparkler burning out its light in the darkness.

Our friendship clearly did not have the same meaning to her as it did to me, and I decided there and then no one would ever gain my solemn friendship again. My heart would not be broken twice. I would guard and protect it always. On the last day of term, we all wrote final good-luck messages to one another in our school books. I got the girls to write their messages in my hymnbook. I often look at that book and read the farewell pledges of so-called friendship and wonder whatever happened to the girls who wrote them. For when we left school, all ties ended. They went their way and I went mine.

Life in the outside world, away from the security of the school walls, was going to be different. Mixed-colour friendships were looked down upon. You "stayed with your own kind" and it was not socially acceptable to mix with another culture. Janice's betrayal, and the end of school life, had certainly made that clear to me.

CHAPTER TWELVE

I was due to start work at Barclays Bank in September. So at the end of my final term I was prepared to spend the summer as usual helping Marmie take care of my younger brothers and sister, making sure they were kept happy during the long holidays.

To break the monotony, Marmie would take us on day trips to the seaside or on picnics in the countryside. She always took us on exciting trips – not just in the summer but all through the year. The ones I remember particularly affectionately were during our Easter holidays when we went to see the grand Easter parade at Battersea Park in London, with its huge decorative floats and the amazing Easter-bonnet competitions.

We never went to restaurants, but I loved going to Hampton Court to sit by the river, where we'd eat our scrummy tucks. At that time we didn't go away on holidays, so the day trips were a real treat for us.

But, quite unexpectedly, on the first day of that year's summer holidays, a girl called Joan – who I was not particularly friendly with at school – came round to my house with her mum. To my amazement, she had come to ask Marmie if I could go away on holiday for two weeks with her and her family, to Dorset. They were going camping and would like me to join them. I knew she was only being friendly with me because she fancied my handsome brother Lester. I'm sure she would have preferred him to go instead, but this was her way of getting close to him.

To my surprise, Marmie said yes. I was astounded, because she had never allowed any of us to go away without her before. Perhaps it was because of the cruel treatment we had received when she left us back in Trinidad, I don't know. But she had never even let us join the Girl Guides or Boy Scouts. She always used to say, "You can't trust a soul with your children," and she was very protective.

Anyway, this time somehow it was different. Perhaps she had decided I could take care of myself, or maybe it was the fact that Joan's father worked at the school. Whatever the reason, I was happy to go; I had never been camping before or even been away on a family holiday. So this sounded like a wonderful adventure. Sleeping under the stars at night was something I could only imagine – I couldn't wait to experience it.

We travelled down by car to Charmouth in Dorset and set up camp near the seaside. To my disappointment I didn't take to camping readily, and having to live with almost total strangers wasn't easy, especially as we were all crammed together in a large family tent, which had paper-thin partitions separating the sleeping areas. Joan and I shared one of these areas.

Our sleeping-bags barely covered our bodies when we tucked into them, as we were both tall for our age, and the ground we lay on was damp from the rain which fell most days. I didn't see as many stars as I'd hoped as it was mostly cloudy at night, and when it rained the pitter-pattering of the raindrops would keep me awake and annoy me. But not half as much as Joan's questions about Lester. She was fascinated – besotted – by him.

Before I went to bed I had to make sure I didn't drink too much so I wouldn't need to go to the toilet, because it was a long way to the bathroom, which was in a white concrete building with sand on the floor brought in from the beach. Each morning we would queue up to use the toilets along with the other campers, taking our own toilet paper with us. Then we would wash in the communal washing area in cold water.

Our meals were cooked on a Camping Gaz stove, and the smell of sausages, eggs and bacon first thing in the morning would whet my appetite. Joan's mum would dish out the breakfast on enamel plates and I would scrape every last scrap of food off the plate, especially when she served baked beans with the fry-up.

The few sunny days we had were spent on the beach, frolicking in the cold water, splashing, laughing and having fun. But as I couldn't swim, I never ventured far out into the sea and always made sure I could feel the sand under my feet. I was afraid to put my head under the water and hated getting my hair wet.

I was good at building sandcastles, though. I would dig deep down into the moist sand as possible as though I was searching for treasure, to get as much sand as possible to use for my creative constructions. I was always sad to leave them behind as I knew the sea would come in and wash them away.

After just over a week by the sea, Joan's parents announced that we were going to move on and camp at her grandparents' home near Bournemouth. They had a large garden so the tent fitted easily into it.

Our new site was more homely, as we didn't have to share the facilities with dozens of other people. Meals were shared in the traditional family way around the table, and everything was done to make me feel at home. However, it turned out to be the most embarrassing week of my life.

I started to notice that each time I walked into a room in Joan's grandparents' house, everyone would stop talking. They seemed to hold their breath and give each other little sideways glances. I knew it wasn't because of my colour – Joan wouldn't have asked me on holiday if her family had had racist views. It was a reaction I myself had caused, something about me, but I couldn't help it. Or rather, I suppose I could have avoided this reaction if I had been more careful and not packed in such a hurry when I left home. I should have made sure I had the most important travel necessity in my wash bag.

Living outdoors in the sea air had disguised it, but now in an enclosed space it was only too obvious – especially after almost two weeks without protection. I had forgotten to pack my deodorant, the thing that safeguarded me from giving out a pungent smell caused by my overactive teenage glands, which made everyone in nose-shot recoil.

It was as if they could smell me coming even before I entered the room. This was a new experience for me, and I had to dig deep to overcome the mortifying feeling I was carrying around which undermined my confidence. Normally, each morning at home, after having a wash I would religiously spread the thick white Mum deodorant cream under my armpits and it would give me all-day protection. But while we were camping, even though I scrubbed under my armpits until they almost bled, the bad odour would not go away. I could even smell myself.

But no one said anything; they were too polite, being very British. "Oh, why didn't I pack my Mum deodorant?" I cried to myself. I had no money, so I couldn't go out and buy any, and I was too embarrassed to ask anyone to lend me some. I just had to bide my time and sweat it out – literally.

I had imagined the holiday would be a wonderful adventure – like those I had seen in films at the Saturday-morning pictures in Penge, where campers had great adventures, full of fun and laughter, singing songs and roasting chestnuts in the twilight. This was not the reality. For this camper it was an episode of complete and utter embarrassment and humiliation.

I wished the final days of my camping trip would come quicker than they did. I wanted to be back home with my own family; I just wanted to curl up and die. I spent most of the end of my first holiday outside, away from the crowd – which I'm sure they appreciated.

My overactive teenage glands did settle down, but I vowed never to travel anywhere without my deodorant ever again.

CHAPTER THIRTEEN

Going to work in the City, the financial hub of London, was daunting. I didn't have my ex-friend Janice to go to work with as planned, so I was alone. I took the train from Anerley to London Bridge, like all the other City commuters, and walked the rest of the way to Cannon Street.

The huge office block I worked in was called Bucklersbury House and it was Barclays' Chief Accountant's Office, where the accounts of branches across the country were sent, so that the bank would know how much business had taken place daily. The records would then be sent by messenger to the Bank of England, a stone's throw away from the office where I worked. Even though Barclays Bank had employed me, in those days people of colour were not given jobs as cashiers dealing with the public. We were put behind the scenes, hidden from view. Perhaps the bosses thought we would contaminate the money or lose them customers.

Whatever the reason, I was grateful for the job anyway. At least I wasn't cleaning the office like my mother; I would be helping to support the family by doing a white-collar job in a bank. I was part of the new generation of Caribbeans who were pushing the boundaries and fighting for a place in British society.

The office I worked in was a huge open-plan

space with large mechanical adding machines on the desks. They had big number buttons, and at the side were levers to operate them. I sat at a desk along with seven other people, four of us on each side.

Facing me were young men all dressed in black suits with white shirts and dark-coloured ties – the uniform for young city slickers. All the women dressed in either grey or navy-blue dresses or skirts with white blouses. So in this sombre landscape I really stood out, because I wore colourful clothes – like the mustard-coloured suit Marmie had made Sandra for her job interview. After a while, when I got to know everyone in the office better, I tried to persuade the men to wear coloured shirts and the women to introduce some pastel shades into their attire. Eventually they did so and the office began to look a lot less drab. Some of the girls even started wearing miniskirts – but I liked to be different from the crowd, so I plumped for wearing maxis.

However, I did start a revolution in the City in the way women dressed. One momentous day I turned up at the office wearing a trouser suit. It was the most outrageous thing I could have done, because at that time women never wore trousers to work. Deep down I think the women in the office were glad, because not long afterwards they started following my trend.

Only one person didn't take to my individualism and always made derisive comments. But I just smiled. I wasn't going to let him stifle me, even though he was second-in-command of my department.

I really loved working in the Chief Accountant's Office. I adored dealing with figures, so much so that I decided to abandon my dream of becoming a teacher. My new ambition was to become Britain's first black woman bank manager. I was already going to night classes to take my A levels and I also took a banking diploma, part one.

Another reason I felt so at home at the bank was that I was their Victrix Ludorum, their athletics champion. I had continued my running and joined the Athletics Club. I represented the bank at various championship meetings and I never lost a race. At one meeting in Eastbourne, an athletics coach recommended that I join an established athletics club to train regularly, and suggested that one day I could represent Britain at the Olympics. The idea didn't appeal to me as I didn't enjoy training. (This was partly because I ran naturally and never allowed anyone to overtake me.) To tell you the truth, the main reason I hated it was that it made my legs look too masculine – my thighs bulged like a weightlifter's and I hated that.

But I had no negative thoughts about my job. I really looked forward to each day I spent at the bank and I couldn't wait to go to work. I never missed a day. In the morning I would hurriedly get dressed, rush downstairs and swallow my breakfast, dial the speaking clock (known as TIM) for a time check, then sprint off to the station, giving myself just enough time to catch the train. I suppose that was my way of doing a bit of training.

One particular morning, my skirt needed ironing, so I came downstairs with my maxi coat on and plugged in the iron, which was in the kitchen. While it was heating up I went through my usual routine, then rushed out of the door. It was only when I stepped off the train at London Bridge that I felt a cold draught around my legs. I looked down – and to my horror realized that I didn't have my skirt on! The idea of turning back and missing a day's work never occurred to me; instead I spent the whole day in the office wearing one of the cleaner's pink nylon coats, which the woman in charge of my section gave me to wear. She spared me huge embarrassment that day – but that nylon coat was one fashion item no one copied!

When someone in the office had a birthday or was leaving, it was customary to sign a card and buy cakes or go for a drink after work. I loved the sticky iced buns and the flaky custard slices that squirted out their creamy filling when you bit into them, but I wasn't so keen on going down to the pub because I didn't drink alcohol. The only time I did have something to drink was at home at Christmas. I would have a few sips of cider and almost immediately start crying like a baby and falling over uncontrollably. All the family would laugh and tease me, but Marmie would hug me and comfort me until the alcohol wore off.

I was always full of energy and never needed to drink alcohol to feel good or to dance the night away. Everyone who did drink would change their character and behaviour and the next morning they wouldn't remember what had happened the night before. But I always did, and I could never understand the point of drinking alcohol.

So when I did go drinking with my work colleagues I would order an orange juice, just to be sociable. There was one particular chap who used to tease me about only drinking soft drinks, and on one of these occasions he thought it would be rather funny to spike my orange juice with vodka. At the time I just thought my drink tasted a bit odd and thought nothing more of it. But then suddenly the world seemed to be spinning around and my ears popped like balloons. My knees went weak and I hit the floor with an almighty bang.

The next thing I knew I was waking up in the medical centre back at the office and I felt as though I was dying. I could hear muffled voices but couldn't react. I felt like a rag doll with no control over my floppy limbs. I was in such a state that arrangements had to be made for someone to take me home by taxi, and I was so ill I remained on my sick-bed for three days, unable to move. Marmie was furious about what had happened and so too was my boss, who reprimanded the culprit severely. He was never that foolish again. To this day alcohol has the same effect on me.

CHAPTER FOURTEEN

If I had to choose a favourite age it would be seventeen. It was the age when academic pressure had eased off, when I found myself no longer a child but not yet an adult. Although I was working and going to night classes, I was in a sort of no man's land without any major responsibilities. It was an age when no decisions needed to be made about my immediate future – it was already decided.

At seventeen I felt a certain lightness in my body, a feeling I wished would last for ever. I didn't want to be eighteen, to become an adult. I also had a strange belief that I would not live beyond the age of twenty-one which meant, in my mind, I only had four years to live. So I tried really hard to slow down each day in that eighteenth year. I was determined to enjoy every second, every minute, every hour, every day. I remember smiling constantly as I bathed myself in life's richness.

Marmie had given Sandra and me a little more freedom and allowed us to go places on our own, as long as she approved of where we were going. Our visits to the West Indian Students' Centre in Earls Court did get her consent. "If you go there you will be associating with decent, intelligent young people like yourselves," she said proudly.

We would take the train to Victoria and then the underground to Earls Court. If anyone tried to approach us, Sandra and I would communicate in our own made-up language, which only we could understand. We would pretend we didn't speak English, which always worked. It was so funny to hear what people said about us when they thought we couldn't understand what they were saying. Oh, that made us laugh out loud when we left the train.

I did have to speak out once to someone on a packed train, though. Being a commuter I was accustomed to bodies being unceremoniously squashed together and I did make allowances for this. However, on this occasion I became aware of a hand caressing my bottom. I turned to the owner of the straying hand, looked him in the eye and said in a loud voice, "Excuse me, I don't remember giving you permission to touch my bottom. So stop it!"

He turned beetroot-red and froze with guilty embarrassment as everyone looked at him. At the next stop, he made a hasty exit as soon as the doors opened. I'm sure after that he thought twice before trying the same thing again.

The West Indian Students' Centre was jointly owned by the various West Indian governments and was opened by Princess Margaret in 1955. It was at 1 Collingham Gardens, a large, imposing red-brick building with huge rooms. One was a ballroom with a wooden sprung floor where dances and parties were held. There was also a well-stocked library and several meeting rooms.

Many eminent Caribbean Prime Ministers, politicians, artists, philosophers and writers such as C. L. R. James visited the Centre, and Caribbean students flocked there hungrily searching for intellectual stimulation, as it was a place not just for social activities but where great debates were held as well.

Once Stokely Carmichael, a compatriot of the assassinated civil-rights leader Malcolm X, paid a visit and gave a lecture during the time of the Black Power movement. Malcolm X was known as the father of Black Power and there was a tidal wave of opinion and reaction around the world, mainly from people in America, Britain and the Caribbean who wanted to decide what we were to be called. Up until then we were called anything from "negro", "sambo", "coon", "wog" or "coloured" to the disgusting "n" word – all names decided by people other than our own race.

At the 1968 Olympics in Mexico City the American gold and bronze 200 metre medallists, Tommie Smith and John Carlos, each put on a black glove. They bowed their heads when the Stars and Stripes was raised in the medal ceremony and they straightened their gloved hands in the air. It was a signal for change, a turning-point for many. It was a symbol of free-dom, of being in control and not being afraid of our colour. It was an action that would inspire people of colour around the world.

A song was recorded called "Say it Loud – I'm Black and I'm Proud" by James Brown, which we all learnt by heart and did indeed sing out loud. It was during that time that we overwhelmingly decided "black" was the only acceptable descrip-tion we would tolerate. The descriptive iden-tity "black" was not decided by others. It was our decision. This was a seminal moment in the lives of the descendants of enslaved Caribbean and American people. I certainly felt liberated and uplifted and I was proud to be called "black".

The Students' Centre was a magnet for young Caribbean people who wanted to feel valued and respected. It was one of the few places where we could go and feel socially accepted, a place where we weren't stared at. I joined the organ-izing committee and soon became chair because no one else wanted the responsibility. I used my organizing and motivational skills to arrange social events.

The day trips Marmie had taken us on had influenced me greatly, so I organized coach trips. One memorable one was to the coastal town of Margate. I had made sure it wasn't a Bank Holiday weekend, because I had seen scenes of mayhem in 1964, when swarms of suited mods on their scooters and leather-clad rockers on their motorbikes had descended on seaside towns to wreak havoc and fight their tribal battles. I didn't want us to get caught up in the middle of their confrontations as they would have almost certainly turned on us.

The excursion was quite an experience. We walked around the town and picnicked on the beach, and judging by their reaction I'm not sure if the locals had ever seen a group like us before. From the way they looked at us it must have been a first for them. The sight of two dozen or more West Indians in town must have seemed like an invasion. I'm sure they breathed a sigh of relief when we left, although they never showed us any animosity. They just stared at us as though we were freaks.

The Miss Caribbean beauty contest the committee organized always pulled in a crowd. The prize money would attract the young female students, who would have to parade up and down the middle of the ballroom in evening dress as well as in swimwear, and give a short speech about themselves.

Most of the girls did it in a very amateurish way, copying what they had seen on television in the Miss World beauty competition. But at one contest there was one girl who was far more professional than the others. She knew just how to influence the judges, who were all Caribbean High Commissioners. She was far more developed than the other girls and walked with a swagger that turned heads. Her swimsuit was far too revealing, we all thought. I was the compère, and when I asked her questions about herself she let slip that she was a professional model and was promptly disqualified.

The many dances I organized at the Centre were always a sell-out. The girls would dress in their shortest minis. Their hair would either be combed in a voluminous Afro – "natural" – or be straightened and curled.

The process of straightening black hair was a lengthy and complex one. A brass comb would be heated on a gas ring, then used to straighten out sections of tightly curled hair which made it easier to style. The smoke from the burning hair would leave a smelly grey cloud that lingered in the room. The hot comb didn't hurt unless the hairdresser accidentally touched your scalp or ears with it; only then would it leave its mark. When all the hair was straightened, a pair of heated curling tongs would be used to make bouncy curls.

This straightening process was worth going through, because tugging a comb through a mass of naturally tight black curly hair was something you had to summon up all your courage to do. It was so painful it brought tears to your eyes. So the monthly ritual of "pressing" your hair, as it was called, was definitely worthwhile.

The only problem with straightened hair was that at a dance it would frizzle up tightly because of the humidity from the body heat and sweat in the room. This was not good, as the main idea of going to all this trouble was to attract male attention. Fortunately the lights were kept low, but by midnight all straightened hair had reverted back to its original curly state.

The targets of our attention at these dances had abandoned the zoot suits their fathers wore for shirts and trousers with check jackets or slim-cut mohair suits from Burton's. One particular boy always looked great in his stylish attire and had the choice of any girl he fancied. You could always tell when he entered the room because he smelt as though he had poured a whole bottle of Brut aftershave over himself. If he danced with you his aroma would stay with you for at least a week. He danced with me once and I shall never forget the experience. I liked dancing to my own rhythm but he had other ideas. Even though the music we were dancing to had a fast beat, he held me firmly around my waist, drew me close to him and danced slowly to ensure our bodies moved to the same rhythm, and that his scent was left all over me, like a dog marking his patch.

* * *

115

Each year at the Students' Centre we held a carnival dance to remind us of our Caribbean culture. Steel-band music was played and the unique rhythms of the Trinidadian instruments filled the ballroom and made us feel as if we were back on our islands in the sun.

Carnival in Trinidad had started during slavery when the enslaved people dressed up and mimicked their slave masters as a form of amusement. It took place as a celebration just before Lent. It continues today but has evolved into a three-day international spectacular, which still takes place just before Lent and draws revellers in their droves from all over the world.

Carnival celebrations in Britain were started in 1959 by a woman called Claudia Jones, to help Caribbeans facing racism feel comforted by celebrating their culture. The first carnivals were held in big halls like St Pancras Town Hall where people would dress up in fancy costumes to "play mas" and indulge in their music and cultural traditions. They became so popular they were turned into a street carnival; the first one took place in 1964 in Notting Hill, not before Lent but on August Bank Holiday when it was warmer. It has developed into the world-famous Notting Hill Carnival which now attracts millions of people annually.

Our carnival dance was held at the same time as Trinidad's, an annual get-together we never missed. The music everyone enjoyed dancing to at that time was soul music. James Brown was the King of Soul and his records and those by the Four Tops, the Temptations and Aretha Franklin were requested over and over again. I would dance to this music for hours, whether I had a partner or not.

I always looked stylish in whatever I wore when I went dancing, but I was not well endowed when it came to my bust line. So I would stuff sponge enhancers, which I had bought at Woolworth's, into my size 32A bra to try to make it look as though I was at least a 32B. Unfortunately, my secret was discovered during one of my energetic dancing sessions when someone asked me what the strange objects on my chest were. I looked down and saw to my horror that the creamy white peaked sponge enhancers had risen out of position and were sticking to my brown sweaty body. I quickly stuffed them back into position, hoping not too many people had noticed my attempt to appear voluptuous.

Even though I enjoyed every minute of dancing I always felt sad at the end of the evening. I was sad because as the DJ announced the last dance, which was always a slow one, the would-be Casanovas would rush over and grab the desirable partner they had been eyeing up all evening to smooch with. I was never chosen and had to sit on the sidelines like a wallflower, looking on.

CHAPTER FIFTEEN

I have always had a mind of my own and love being independent and not having to rely on anyone. One of the best feelings of independence was when I passed my driving test, but learning to drive was quite an adventure.

The first thing I did on my quest to get my licence was to buy a car.

Most of the money I was earning at that time I gave to Marmie. At the end of each month I would bring home my pay packet and give it to her. She would give me my travel allowance and what she thought would be enough for me to have as spending money. I had opened a bank account and saved a small amount each month. I didn't spend much on food because I took sandwiches to work – sometimes I would sit and eat them on the steps of St Paul's Cathedral, which was near my office, and watch the world go by. Marmie had taught me how to make my own clothes, so I was not extravagant in any way.

Eventually, I had enough money saved for a car, and Dardie suggested I look in *Exchange and Mart* magazine to find one. He came along with me to give support and, thanks to his expert mechanical advice, I purchased a light-blue Austin A35 which he gave the once-over. I paid the owner the huge sum of thirty pounds and Dardie drove it home for me.

I couldn't afford driving lessons, so Marmie decided she would teach me to drive. In fact, she taught all six of us to drive. Dardie had no patience as an instructor and would continually tell us what a great driver he was and that we were doing it all wrong. We would be certain to come back home after a few minutes of being taught – or lectured more like it – by Dardie.

Now my problem was I didn't always know my right from my left when it came to manoeuvring the car. I would think left but turn the steering wheel right. This was a very dangerous trait to have, and looking back I think Marmie was very brave to sit in my snug little car with me at the controls. Unlike the dual-control driving-school cars, she had no way of stopping or controlling the car herself.

One spring evening while it was still light, she had taken me out for a lesson. It was just before the end of the rush hour. I had done a few hill starts and successfully completed a three-point turn, so I was feeling rather pleased with myself as we drove along the main road back to our house.

As we approached the traffic lights at the crossroads, Marmie gave me the command to turn right. I put my hand out of the car and signalled that I was turning. (This was the normal procedure; in those days it was unusual to have indicators on cars.) I began to rotate the steering wheel – but in the wrong direction.

"I said turn right," said Marmie, with a sound of alarm in her voice. "Turn right! Right!" she screamed.

I suddenly realized I was turning the wheel in an anticlockwise direction and swung it clockwise like a racing driver on a rally, wheels screeching, tyres burning. I just missed the traffic lights as I took a deep sweep to the right, mounting the pavement and coming down with a bump, our heads hitting the roof and my little A35 rattling our bodies.

All Marmie said was, "Child, you trying to kill us? Just slow down."

Yes, Marmie was a very brave instructor and together we experienced lots of other hair-raising incidents before I mastered the art of driving and remembered my right from my left. I'm so grateful she stuck with me because eventually, after three disastrously unsuccessful attempts, I finally passed my driving test. The first time I took the test, it was such a frightening experience for the examiner that when we had completed it he simply said, "Young lady, until you can learn to take your foot off the accelerator, don't come back."

By sheer coincidence, I had the same examiner on my fourth test. When we had completed the test, I gently brought the car to a halt and waited anxiously for the result, hoping I had completed my mission and the examiner would reward me with that elusive passport to independence, my driving licence. He didn't say a word, but continued to scratch away furiously with his pen for what seemed to be for ever.

My heart began to quicken, the anxiety swelling up inside me. I couldn't bear to fail again, as I was becoming the butt of everyone's jokes at home.

Eventually he looked over at me, his expression not giving anything away, and said, "It's obvious to me, young lady, that you have finally taken my advice and stopped using the highway as a Formula 1 race track. I'm pleased to say that today you have passed with flying colours."

I was the happiest girl alive for I suddenly got a feeling of true independence.

Soon after that, I sold my faithful little Austin A35 for ten pounds to a scrap-metal dealer. My little jalopy and I had been through some "challenging encounters", and it could take no more. I then bought myself a pale-yellow and white Ford Anglia and I drove it less dramatically. Well, sometimes.

CHAPTER SIXTEEN

By 1967 three of us had left school. Lester was the next to go to work. He left school at fifteen to start an apprenticeship as an electrician. Twenty-five years later he went on to be a mature student and passed his Master's in engineering with a first, which only goes to show it's never too late to learn. Today he is responsible for the upkeep of one of the country's most important and historic buildings.

Dardie was now an accounts clerk at British Rail as well as still playing gigs at weekends, and with Marmie's earnings as a baby-minder and three extra wage packets coming in, things were looking good. So with the financial situation getting better at home, Marmie decided to upgrade and climb further up the property ladder. Finally she felt we could afford to buy a bigger house, with a garden. She loved gardening and missed not having her own green patch like the one we'd had in Trinidad, where she grew everything from beautiful exotic flowers to vegetables and herbs.

The small three-bedroom terraced house we had owned for the past seven years in Anerley did not have a proper garden, just a tiny concrete backyard with an outside toilet as a main feature. Before buying it, when we first arrived in England we had rented a room in someone else's house, all eight of us in one tiny room. Two months later we had moved into two larger rooms. Marmie was determined, after our cramped, unhappy, restricted experiences, that we would live in a whole house as a family, without a lodger – unlike most West Indian families who rented out rooms in their homes. She wanted us to feel free, to live alone in our own house as we had in Trinidad. And not in an area where many other Caribbeans lived either, because she believed that way we would get the best education, healthcare and jumble sales.

At that time it was almost impossible for Caribbeans to borrow money from a bank, as they were not considered to be trustworthy customers. So they had to find creative ways of raising money and developed something called a su su or partner, which worked like this: a group of friends would put in, say, ten pounds each week. One of them would be given the pot to buy whatever they were saving for, and each person would take their turn to receive the pot.

Marmie joined a su su and that was how, after just a year of our being in England, she had been able to put the £100 deposit down on the house in Anerley, which cost £1,000. Amazingly, this included all the furniture, carpets, curtains and even the cutlery. We were so lucky as this was very unusual.

This time she had set her sights on a bigger

semi-detached house with a garden in the afflu-ent middle-class area of Beckenham in Kent. She arranged for us to view it on a Sunday afternoon and so we piled into the Zephyr, leaving Dardie at home practising his saxophone. Marmie drove up outside the house, which had a large "For Sale" sign rooted in the front garden. It looked very big and impressive compared with the one we were living in, and we were all thrilled at the prospect of living there. The street was wide and empty and the gardens looked neat and well kept, full of shrubs and roses.

The lace curtains in the windows of the other houses looked fresh and clean. We could see a few of them being slightly pulled aside, but thought nothing of it. We ran up the path to the front door and Marmie opened it with the key the estate agent had given her. The empty house looked as big as a palace and we scrambled from room to room, almost hysterical with excite-ment as we decided who was going to have which bedroom. Yes, we were definitely upgrading.

Suddenly a loud commotion outside cut through our laughter. We looked out of the uncurtained windows and could see flashing lights. The street was now full of green and white panda cars, Black Maria vans and police motorbikes. We were surrounded by the law, like hunted criminals – a woman and six children, at 2.30 p.m. on a Sunday afternoon.

The first policeman to come up the long path was dressed in puffed-out black leather trousers and wearing a crash helmet and goggles. Marmie opened the door and greeted him with a smile. When he saw her he smiled back and turned to the other officers. "Leave this to me," he said in a voice of authority. "I will deal with them."

Reluctantly they got back into their vehicles and drove off. The policeman took off his helmet and came into the house; we all stepped aside as he passed by and trailed after him into the empty living room.

"What can I do for you, officer?" asked Marmie.

"We've had reports from several of the neighbours that a large group of hooligans have broken into the house to steal," he said, looking round at the empty room.

"Now I understand why almost the whole local police force came out to arrest us," said Marmie, laughing.

The thought of our viewing the house to buy it was obviously far beyond the neighbours' imaginations. We wondered why the policeman was so understanding and had stopped the other police officers arresting and interrogating us. He explained that he was married to a Ghanaian doctor and they lived just a few streets away with their children. The same thing had happened to his wife when she went to view the house they now lived in.

Marmie was not angered, frightened or put off by the incident. She had set her heart on moving up the property ladder and no amount of pressure was going to stop her. We bought the house, and its large garden became her pride and joy. The flowers bloomed and she seemed to have special green fingers that made everything she touched thrive.

Sadly, though, our neighbours were hostile and abusive towards us and many of them moved out – except for the Italian family who lived next door. Before the Caribbeans arrived in Britain, the Italians had been the last to emigrate here in numbers and had experienced similar adversities. So they were very sympathetic.

As for the police officer, he and his wife became friends of ours. He used to tell us tales of what some of his fellow police officers thought of Caribbean people and the derogatory names some of them called us. Eventually, he could no longer stomach the prejudice and left the police force, realizing he couldn't fight institutional injustice on his own.

Marmie wasn't going to give up, though. She stood her ground and lived there in our beloved family home, for over forty years, until she died there in 2008. When I became a baroness, I decided to honour Marmie by choosing the title Baroness Benjamin of Beckenham.

CHAPTER SEVENTEEN

We had no white friends when we left school and only mixed socially with other Caribbean people. At that time there were not many people from Africa, India or Pakistan living in Britain, so we stuck to our own culture.

Sandra, Lester and I were a team and we went everywhere together and looked out for one another. But they couldn't drive, so they depended on me for transport at weekends.

We didn't go out during the week as we busied ourselves with further studies at night classes. So Saturday night was party time, the time to celebrate the end a long working week. All day would be spent planning our entertainment. Lester had made two friends at work who were also doing apprenticeships, and they became part of our Saturday gang. Sandra and I had made friends with a girl called Anita who we had met at the West Indian Students' Centre. She became almost like a sister to us and so she partied with us too. There wasn't always a dance on at the Students' Centre but between us there was always the likelihood of someone knowing of a house party. If we didn't know the exact address, I would drive around with the windows open and everyone else would have their heads out of the packed car, listening anxiously for music which would alert us to where the house party was. Then we would follow the trail to where the sound was coming from.

At the house party there would usually be a small fee to pay at the door, and the drinks would also have to be paid for – but as none of us drank, that didn't bother us. We were there for the dancing.

The music would be pumped out loud through huge speakers. The sounds of ska, rock steady and soul pulsated, the deeply thunderous bass made your heart thump and feel as if it was about to burst out of your chest. All the rooms would be packed and humid with fun-seeking bodies moving as one, gyrating to the heavy beat. Sandra and Anita attracted the boys, both of them having scores of admirers who clamoured to dance with them, but it was not the same for me. I danced alone.

Once, an American soldier, who had somehow found himself together with a friend at a house party we were at, took pity on me and asked me to dance. I'm sure it was because he felt out of it too and I was the only girl without a partner. He was from Chicago and was over in England serving on a US base in Berkshire, and had come to London on leave.

He asked me out – and I immediately listed the conditions on which I would accept his offer. "I don't kiss, hold hands or allow hanky-panky!"

I said haughtily. "Do you still want to go out with me?"

To my surprise he said, "Yes," in his cool American drawl. I think he must have found me a challenge.

I laid out these conditions because another boy had tried it on once when I had given him a lift home after night school, since he lived near me. When we pulled up outside his house he leaned over and tried to kiss me.

I'm not sure if it was my friendliness that gave him the idea that I was easy prey, but whatever it was I had to defend myself. I was trapped in a sitting position, however, and couldn't take a good swing at him. The only defence I had was my car, which I used to my advantage.

As he slowly leaned towards me, his eyes closed, his lips pouted ready for action, I began to panic. He was serious and getting ever closer. I knew I had to do something, so in a moment of madness, to avoid his amorous advances I swiftly inserted my head into the steering wheel, clasping my arms around it to protect myself. Then, trying to take complete charge of the situation from my refuge, I ordered him in the best-controlled tones I could muster, "Get out of my car!"

There was silence; no word was uttered by my suitor. I couldn't see his face, so I didn't know how my unexpected reaction to his advances had affected him, nor did I want to engage in an embarrassing confrontation. So I didn't surface again until I heard the door slam. Then I promptly drove home, thankful for my lucky escape.

My American friend was not so forward. He was a perfect gentleman and bought Sandra, Anita and me gifts every time he met us. The one I treasured most was a comb-and-brush set which came in a beautiful padded gift box. The brush, which had a gold-trimmed handle, sat snugly in the blue satin fabric alongside the hand mirror with its cream and gold embroidered back. I never used the set, but kept it as a precious gift. Nor did I ever let him hold my hand or kiss me; I left that to his imagination. He might have been biding his time, but it ran out because he was called back to America and I never saw him again.

I may not have been good at boyfriend/girlfriend relationships myself, but I was the perfect matchmaker. I would find the right partners for everyone in our gang. Perhaps it was because I liked observing and studying people and enjoyed making them feel happy. But Dardie was beginning to wonder if I was a bit "strange". I once overheard him asking Marmie, with a note of concern in his voice, "Do you think Floella is a zammie tess?" That's Caribbean for a lesbian. "She's eighteen and not had a boyfriend yet."

"No," said Marmie. "She'll find out what it's all about in her own time."

Marmie was right. I was going to wait to release my caged heart and allow it to nestle in the field of love. What I was certain about was that the key to free my heart would be in the hands of someone who would be gallant, charming, patient, loyal, brave and funny all wrapped up in kindness. Someone who would love, cherish and protect me through thick and thin. But at that time I was too busy arranging other people's lives and taking care of them.

Mind you, one night I almost ended the lives of some of my nearest and dearest. We had been to a party near Ladbroke Grove in west London, where we'd had a great time. As usual I was driving and the car was packed with the gang. There were not many other cars on the road, so I drove as though I was on a race track. I roared down Park Lane and hardly braked as I entered Hyde Park Corner. I screeched round the bend on two wheels, with the car almost turning over.

Next thing I knew, a police car pulled up alongside me and told me to stop. I didn't realize that they had been tracking me for about a mile. The policeman came to my side of the car and said, "Right, sir, out of the car." When he saw me he said, "Blimey, it's a girl!"

I knew by this reaction that he was taken aback, so I took advantage of his surprise by acting innocently. "What can I do for you, officer?" I said sweetly.

Instead of throwing the book at me, he gave me a long lecture. "If you want to kill yourself, fine, but don't take all your friends with you. Now, just slow down and drive home safely," he said in a fatherly tone.

"Yes, sir," I said sheepishly.

Marmie had told us to always be polite to police officers if they stopped us. I knew I was in the wrong and would have made the situation worse if I had argued or been rude to him. So I got back into the car and drove home as sedately as I could, treating my passengers as if they were fragile pieces of china. I'm not sure I would have got away with just a telling-off from a traffic cop today. But that night, because of the police officer's lecture I learnt I had to modify my behaviour and have a more responsible attitude to my driving.

CHAPTER EIGHTEEN

Apart from my two-week camping trip, which was an utter disaster, I still hadn't been away on a proper holiday. So in 1968 Sandra and I excitedly planned our first summer holiday abroad.

A family friend had recommended to Marmie a guest-house near the city of Rotterdam in Holland. He had stayed there himself and told her we would be safe and well cared-for. Even though we were now both over eighteen, in order for us to go we still needed her approval. Fortunately, as the trip met her conditions, we were allowed to go.

So we packed our suitcases till they were almost bursting with our most fashionable clothes, mostly made by Marmie. We were ready for any occasion, day or evening. My favourite dress was a lilac-and-white chequered shift dress which was perfect for my skinny figure. It hung like a cut-out shape of the letter T over my curveless body. I wore white, pointed slingback shoes with it and, if it was sunny, a pair of Ray-Ban sunglasses. When I was dressed like that I felt quite chic. Sandra and I couldn't wait to hit the town.

We took the boat from Harwich to Rotterdam with slight trepidation – the last sea journey we had made, as little girls, had been across the ocean from Trinidad eight years before and we had suffered terribly from seasickness. Luckily we had no such problems this time.

When we arrived at the port, full of excitement at the thought of our impending adventure, the Dutch husband and wife from the guest-house were there waiting for us. They were very sweet and to our relief spoke perfect English. We got into their car, our large suitcases in the back, and drove off. The journey took longer than we had imagined, as we left the busy city behind us and drove into the flat green countryside.

We travelled for miles without seeing any shops, houses or people. We were beginning to get a little concerned, as we were now miles away from any form of activity. Then suddenly the car pulled off the main road, bumped along a mud track and stopped. The smell of manure filled the air as we stepped out, trying to avoid the cow dung in our path.

It turned out the guest-house was on a farm in a village in the middle of nowhere! Sandra and I looked at each other in horror. So much for our "hit the town" holiday. We lugged our heavy suitcases up to our room and went straight to bed under a blanket of disappointment.

And things didn't get any better the next morning: we were woken at the crack of dawn by a chorus of farm animals practising their daily tunes. This made it impossible to sleep, so the thought of food came into our minds; we had not eaten for a while and we were looking forward to breakfast. I loved my food, and to me breakfast was a most important meal. At home we would have some of Marmie's home-made bread, then cereal, followed by bacon and eggs, all washed down with a cup of cocoa. The thought of a hearty breakfast excited my taste-buds. But when we got downstairs, our excitement was halted. To our amazement, the breakfast table looked quite sparse. Where was all the food, I wondered.

I felt puzzled and confused, because in front of us was a white runny mixture with lumps in it – which turned out to be live yoghurt. There was no warm, soft, freshly baked bread, just hard crispbread and a sort of black hard dough bread, with thin squares of cheese and honey on them – and that was it. What a disappointment! But I was starving and had to eat something, so I forced the food down, knowing that it was keeping my hunger at bay. I got no other pleasure from each mouthful, and from the way Sandra looked I was sure she felt the same.

It took us about half an hour to walk around the whole village, which had a few shops – definitely not the sort for window-shopping.

There were no real attractions. But we ourselves became an attraction soon after we arrived. A rumour had gone round that there were two strangers in town, and the news seemed to travel like wildfire. To our amazement, the hundred or more villagers didn't just want to see what we were like, they wanted to touch us too!

The first time it happened we were rather taken aback. Someone rushed up, stroked our skin and rushed off again. This was repeated time and time again over the two weeks we were there. Apparently there was a superstition in the village that if you saw something black you had to touch it, because it would bring you good luck. Come to think of it, Sandra and I should have been lucky all the time since we touched our own black skin constantly! Mind you, I didn't feel very lucky having to spend the whole of our summer holidays in a Dutch backwater where the flat land had been reclaimed from the sea. I wished someone would reclaim *us* and take us back to exciting '60s London.

The only excitement we had was listening to a record we had brought with us. Luckily there was a record-player in the sitting room at the guest-house. It was a box covered in grey vinyl which sat on the sideboard. When you opened the lid, there was a black turntable at the bottom of the box with a thin metal spindle to place the record on. I put my precious record, the first one I had ever bought, on the turntable. Sandra and I loved singing along to it and as we waited for the intro we prepared ourselves to burst into song.

The sound that came out of the record-player was not as good as from the Blue Spot radiogram at home, but it didn't matter. We sang our hearts out to the Supremes' "Baby Love". We knew every word, and we played it so many times, imagining we were on the stage performing, that we almost wore it out.

One evening we were invited to a dance at the village hall and we took the record along with us. We got the whole village dancing to "Baby Love" that night – when the villagers weren't showing off their rather strange party trick. The men all lined up and, one by one, put a live ferret down their trousers. The ferrets had very sharp teeth and would bite anything that moved, so the idea was to see who could keep their ferret in their trousers the longest without moving. That was their idea of entertainment.

Before the end of our holiday we did manage to visit the city of Rotterdam once, when the farmer and his wife arranged for one of their friends, who had a stall in a Rotterdam market, to take us along with him. We were so grateful to escape the village that we grasped this precious opportunity to hit the town with joy.

We left with their friend very early in the morning mist and got to the city by 8 a.m. To our surprise, we had to help him unpack his van and set up his stall. Then, even more worryingly, he boasted to his fellow stallholders that we were his new assistants. We started to get rather nervous about what exactly was expected of us. Surely we didn't have to stay with him all day and work as cheap labour on his stall?

Sandra and I looked at each other helplessly, wondering if we should make a run for it. But how would we get back to the guest-house? We only had a small amount of money and no means of transport. Then, to our relief, at 9 a.m. he told us that everything was now open so we could go and have a good time wandering around the city. But we had to be back by 6 p.m. to return to village life.

We felt as though we were set free as we went around the city, trying to see as much as we could in the short time we had, stopping only to eat chips smothered in mayonnaise which were sold in paper cones from street-corner kiosks. That day I did get the chance to wear my favourite shift dress for the first time on the holiday, and I walked around Rotterdam feeling quite chic.

CHAPTER NINETEEN

As a teenager I often wondered if the world and those around me would ever understand how I sometimes felt. The pressures of the world seemed to weigh heavily on my shoulders. Cruelty, injustice, famine, war and violence all took their toll. Sometimes facing the world at all would seem like a huge burden, especially if high expectations were put upon me.

I knew that many other teenagers had felt this for generations, but it was no consolation. I wished I had the power to change the world, to make it different, but at the time I felt helpless and unable to do so.

As I said before, I never thought I would live beyond the age of twenty-one. I was positive my life would come to an early end, and at that time it seemed to me it would be the natural age for me to die. Looking back forty years later I'm so glad I didn't (if only I had known then what I know now), but I was never afraid of death. At the age of ten, when I was going through the miserable period of living away from my family, I had seen a dead man lying in his coffin. He looked so peaceful, and even though he was in his eighties he looked so young. His face was as smooth as a baby's. Our Italian next-door neighbour had that same look when he died. His family had invited us to come and see him and pay our last respects and, again, even though he was old he looked peaceful and calm as we peered into his open casket. Both men had died a natural death and that's what I thought I would have at twenty-one.

Many teenagers think of committing suicide, but that was not the route for me no matter how hard life seemed to be. If ever I went through a bad period, I would think, "Life is a mixture of bitter and sweet, with ups and downs. The more I go down, the happier I must feel, because the inevitable journey upwards will bring happiness".

One of the saddest things that happened to me probably wouldn't have had the same effect on others, but to me it was like losing part of my soul. It was just after my nineteenth birthday. I had come home from work one evening and saw a bonfire blazing in the garden. It wasn't Guy Fawkes night, so I wondered what it could be. Marmie was stoking the fire.

"What are you doing?" I asked casually.

"I've been spring cleaning and getting rid of some of the rubbish in the house," she said, keeping her eyes on the blaze.

I thought nothing of it until I went into the room I shared with my sisters. As I flopped onto the bed, I noticed that the box I usually had in the corner with all my hoarded school books was gone. Alarm bells rang, and I scrambled down the stairs like a fireman on duty and rushed out to the garden, where the fire was still blazing. "Where are my school books?" I screamed hysterically.

"I told you to tidy your room and clear out your books. Well, I did it for you," said Marmie firmly.

Marmie liked a tidy house and always threw away or destroyed anything she thought was unnecessary. To her, my precious books had served their purpose. I had left school three years ealier, so in her eyes I had no use for them. But I believed part of my life had been destroyed, and all I could do was look at the smouldering ashes and sob. I was so upset by her actions I felt I could have died.

Speaking of dying, I have done some foolish things in my time which could have ended my life prematurely. Like the time when I washed my hair and decided to use the hairdrier to dry it quickly. It was an old-fashioned one which only fitted into the light socket hanging from ceiling. I remember standing on a chair to reach the socket. But as I did so I suddenly wondered what it would be like to put my finger into the socket instead. So as I stood up high, with dripping hair touching my shoulders, I stupidly put my finger into the socket.

What happened next can only be described as a miracle. Instead of being killed instantly, I felt an almighty shock pass through my body.

The force threw me and the hairdrier off the chair onto the carpeted floor. I was lucky to be alive – it was not my time to go. I was only nineteen.

Some teenagers *do* wish their lives were over at this age. It's not to do with excessive curiosity, because of emotional and physical traumas they have been subjected to – in many cases sexual abuse, sometimes by those closest to them at home in what should be a safe, loving environment. Those who have to live through this mental and bodily intrusion often feel the only escape is to turn to drink and drugs, self-harm or even suicide. Despite the fact that it's not their fault.

My parents never put me through that torment. They worshipped their children and cared about our well-being too much. This gave me a feeling of security, the trust all children need in order to flourish and grow, free from deep scarring of the mind.

Confirmation of this was given to me late one night when Dardie came home with one of his fellow musicians after a gig to have a drink, something he did frequently. As I lay in bed, I heard their voices and knew immediately it was the drummer. I often overheard Marmie and Dardie gossiping about him. "I don't know why he likes bringing young girls to the gigs," Dardie would say in a disapproving tone of voice. "Some of them are young enough to be his daughters."

"You should tell him, Roy. I don't know why you don't find yourself a new drummer," Marmie would say.

"A good drummer is hard to find these days, and he's good!"

I never liked the drummer because I knew Marmie didn't. I was conscious of his presence and kept my distance. You couldn't miss him in a crowd, even though he was short, because he was built like a brick wall and had a thick neck. The hands at the ends of his muscular arms had stubby fingers which he tapped rhythmically even when he spoke. He had a conceited look about him and swaggered as he walked, his dark blue coat with a velvet collar draped over his broad shoulders. When he smiled, he flashed his gold teeth, which glistened, and in my head the look on his face was like a fox salivating before sneaking up to prey on defenceless chickens in their coop.

I was surprised when I heard him downstairs, because Dardie had never brought him back to the house late at night before.

When we went to bed at night, we kept our bedroom door slightly ajar to let in the light, so I could hear his laughter and the clink of glasses as he and Dardie chatted about how the gig had gone. I must have dozed off, because the next thing I remember is being awakened by footsteps coming up the stairs. I heard Dardie's hushed voice from below, telling the drummer to be quiet as the phone was on the landing outside our door, and my sisters and I were asleep. Through the slit of the door I could now see his squat, shadowy figure heading towards the telephone. Suddenly he turned, which made me instinctively shrink under my blanket so as not to be seen. Then I heard our door creak, and a wider shaft of light fell across my bed. I could hear the rasping of his breath and a strong smell of alcohol seeped into the room.

Then I heard Dardie's voice, at the top of the stairs now. "What are you doing?" he demanded.

"Let's go in and see your girls, Roy," the drummer whispered conspiratorially.

Like a protective hero, Dardie came back at him fiercely: "What kind of man are you, wanting to interfere with young girls? There is no way I'll ever allow you to touch my daughters." I heard a scuffle as Dardie almost threw him down the stairs. "And from now on you can find another band to play in."

With that, the drummer was bundled out of the house and never allowed back. I never told Dardie what I had heard that night, but I am for ever grateful to him for protecting me from the experience of sexual abuse by a paedophile, which could have scarred me for life. Others are not so fortunate.

But years later I did once find myself in a dangerously vulnerable situation that could also have ended in horror, and this time Dardie wasn't there to protect me. It was one Saturday morning, and my car had developed a problem, which was a disaster, because if it broke down it meant we would not have transport for our Saturday-night party treat. I had to get it fixed or there would be huge disappointment. Unfortunately most garages closed at midday on Saturday, but luckily I found one in Gypsy Hill – in south London, not far from where we lived – which stayed open until late, and the mechanic promised to fix the car for me.

"Come back at 5 p.m.," he said. "I'll have it ready for you."

"Oh, thank you so much," I said with relief. "I am so grateful to you for helping me out."

I arrived back promptly at 5 p.m., only to find the garage closed. I could see my car sitting on the forecourt, but the mechanic was nowhere to be seen.

So I knocked on the metal door, in the hope that he would still be there. "Anyone there?" I cried in desperation.

Suddenly the door creaked open. "Come in," said the mechanic with a friendly smile.

"Oh, thank goodness you're still here," I said, breathing a sigh of relief. "I thought you'd gone."

"I'm still here; I've been waiting for you.

Come through to my office." He led the way across the grease-laden garage floor into a tiny office, which had two chairs and a desk with lots of papers on it.

"So what do I owe you for the car?" I said cheerfully as I sat down and took out my cheque book.

"You!" he said in a chilling voice.

I looked up swiftly and saw a look in his eyes that told me I was in danger. "Pardon?" I said quizzically as though I hadn't quite heard him.

"I want you," he said, with a sound of determination in his voice tinged with excitement. He knew he had his victim trapped with no escape, nowhere to run.

But I didn't panic. I stared back at him and looked him in the eyes for what seemed like for ever. Then I sat up with a straight back in my chair, crossed my legs and clasped my hands together on my lap, the way I had seen my posh English teacher Mrs Thomas behave when she was about to deliver some imperious criticism. That's how she had imposed herself on me, and I was now emulating her persona years later. "Now, now, my good man," I said, in the haughtiest voice I could squeeze from my vocal cords without trembling, "don't be foolish."

"Please let me have you," he said, now with a desperate note in his voice; "I've never had a coloured girl before."

"Well, you're not about to fulfil your fantasy now," I said firmly. "How much do I owe you?"

"Just let me touch you," he pleaded. I came straight back at him with an air of superiority. "My good man, if you so much as lay one finger on me, my three large six-foot brothers will come round and teach you a lesson you will never forget. Now pull yourself together and tell me how much I owe you."

There was a deafening silence and I held my breath, hoping my Mrs Thomas strategy had worked. He leaned slightly forward and then, to my relief, turned to his desk, meek and mild like a disgraced schoolboy, and handed me the bill.

I calmly wrote out a cheque and handed it to him with disdain, keeping my composure. "Now, take me to my car," I commanded as I took my keys off the desk.

I still had the presence of mind to insist he lead the way so I could keep an eye on him. I was right to be cautious, because as he stood up I noticed his flies were open and he was ready for action should he have got his way. The slow journey back through the murky garage seemed endless, as I feared he might turn on me without warning. But finally the scary walk to freedom ended as he opened the small metal door. As the evening sunlight burst in I plunged into it, escaping his menacing presence.

It was only when I got into my car and

slammed the door safely behind me that my emotions got the better of me. My hand trembled as I turned the key in the ignition. I put my foot down hard on the accelerator and flew home like the wind, my heart beating like kettledrums, my whole body vibrating. Tears sprang from my eyes and rolled down my face as I sobbed out loud, like a child longing to be comforted in protective arms. My sense of survival had got me through the ordeal and I had shown no fear at the time, but now my stomach was churning. Fortunately I had been strong enough in the presence of a predator not to show my true emotions. I had stayed in control and had not become a victim.

At that moment, through my tears, I saw quite clearly that many of the episodes I had encountered over the years had helped me to build a foundation that would assist me in a positive way and come to my rescue in times of need. Without realizing it I had developed the art of not showing my true emotions; I had learnt to take charge of a situation and act with confidence without breaking down. I realized that adversities, no matter how harsh, happen for a reason and it was up to me how I coped with them. They could either break my spirit and drive me crazy or make me strong and resilient. I had chosen the latter.

When I got home and told everyone what had happened, we decided it was no use reporting the mechanic. If my brothers had attacked him they would end up facing the law. It would be my word against his. That's how abusers survive; they can't be touched without proof.

CHAPTER TWENTY

It took me a long time to look in the mirror and feel happy with the image that stared back at me.

For years my large features seemed to be the wrong size for my small face. Dardie used to tell me that when he first came to the hospital to see me when I was born, not only was he disappointed that Marmie had produced another girl (he wanted a boy), but also he was taken aback by the way I looked. Apparently when he first saw me I had such big eyes, mouth and nose that they almost covered the whole of my face. As I grew up, I would forever be called "big eyes", because of the giant orbs staring out of my tiny face when I opened them to express my thoughts. I was also called "big nose", because my nostrils looked like tunnels chiselled out of a rock protruding out in front of my face, and "big teeth" because they looked like tombstones in a cemetery, pearly white slabs of ivory stuck in my mouth. My face seemed to carry these oversized necessities for years.

Also for as long as I could remember every patch of my face had always been covered in spots. "Buttons" they called them in Trinidad, and I would get comments like "Lend me some buttons to sew on my shirt" or "You could put the sewing shop out of business with all your buttons."

Sandra and Cynthia had gorgeous skin, hardly a blemish to be seen, and I wished I could look like them. Marmie tried to make us all feel loved and equal. She would praise us and give us compliments to boost our confidence. When we were dressed to go out, she would say, "Sandra, you're so pretty, Cynthia, you are beautiful, and Floella, well ... you are attractive."

Attractive! What does attractive mean? I wondered. I wanted to be pretty or beautiful – I knew what they meant. But by the way Marmie said the word "attractive" I felt it must be something to feel special about, even though I wasn't sure what it meant.

I longed to like what I saw in the mirror when I looked at myself. Because I didn't, I would always stand well back from the glass (apart from when I kissed it, that is), even when I put on my make-up. I didn't like being too close to my reflection. Until one day, like the swan in the ugly-duckling story, I looked in the mirror and it seemed as though everything fitted and my features had slotted into place. My face had finally caught up with the rest of me! I started to like what I saw looking back at me from the mirror.

But, just when I felt comfortable with my looks, disaster struck on a night out in Croydon. It was at a bowling alley, a large Victorian building with a steep, sweeping red-and-gold-carpeted staircase. There were velvet-covered seats dotted around the large room, which was packed with Friday-night revellers who had come bowling to start their weekend enjoyment. There were two bouncers, dressed in black suits, who welcomed people as they entered through the huge glass doors.

A friend and I had gone there, paid our entrance fee at the kiosk and joined the fun and excitement. As usual I was very competitive as we played each game, and I was so engrossed in striking the pins with the huge round ball that I hardly noticed the sea of white faces all around me. I was enjoying the game too much. Every time I made a strike I would jump for joy. My laughter filled the air.

It was a wonderful evening, and as we happily left after the game I felt as though I didn't have a care in the world.

Suddenly, as we made our way up the staircase, I felt myself being lifted from behind by my armpits and launched uncontrollably forward. My mind couldn't make sense of what was happening – were others sharing my euphoria, carrying me aloft in triumph like a winning champion? But from the tone of the voices around me I soon realized this was not a friendly act. With terrifying speed, my legs dangling like a puppet's on a string, my feet crashing into every step, I was hoisted to the top of the staircase, at the mercy of my two attackers.

I looked over and saw my friend was in the same predicament. We couldn't defend ourselves from the group of cowards who were attacking us from behind. Cowards always prowl in packs to pounce on the defenceless. These ones shouted as if they were on an army attack and we were the enemy. As we reached the entrance, they attempted to bundle us through the huge glass doors and we tried to resist, in the hope of being rescued by the bouncers. But to my astonishment they didn't come to our assistance; instead they turned their backs and looked away, standing still like soldiers on guard duty. I watched my friend being thrown to the ground, then bounced off the glass doors, kicked and stamped on by his attackers, who took great pleasure in hurting a defenceless teenager.

I hadn't had a fight for five years now, and the Incredible Hulk-like power I possessed had been put to sleep. I had come to terms with who I was, and nothing anyone could say could rile me up the way it used to before I had what I called my spiritual moment. I had realized that fighting wasn't the way to win – but now I was beginning to have second thoughts.

I knew I was not going to be accepted everywhere I went without some people thinking I had no right to be there. Yes, I was generally accepted at work and was welcomed in that office environment, but socially there were still places where people would find my presence offensive. This bowling alley was one of those places and I had been caught out, exposed. I tried to call up my old super fighting powers as I was being attacked, but nothing came. I screamed at the bouncers to help us, but to my dismay they continued to look ahead like stone statues, as if hypnotized. I realized no SOS would be heard by them that night, no matter how hard I screamed for help as the attackers viciously laid into us. So instead I gave a long piercing scream into the ear of one of my attackers, which seemed to anger him: he turned and looked at me with blind hatred in his eyes. Then he leaned back as though he was about to do the shotput. His closed fist came hurtling towards me like a rocket, yet in my mind it seemed like slow motion and I froze in disbelief. His clenched fist slammed into my mouth and my face shuddered from the force of the blow. His knuckles rammed their way between my lips, knocking out one of my tombstone teeth and causing blood to spurt from my mouth. "Take that, you f***ing n**ger," he spat with venomous hatred.

I reeled as the salty taste of my tears mixed with the flavour of fresh blood in my mouth made me realize the ferocity of the violence that was penetrating my soul. I felt my tooth fly towards the back of my throat and, with reawakened quick reactions, I grabbed it and stuck it back into place in my gum. As I held it there, the warm red liquid dribbled down my arm. I had never shed blood like this before and suddenly I became nauseous and light-headed. My lips throbbed and felt like blown-up marshmallows stuck to my face, but I forced myself to keep pressing on my tooth as I had seen someone do that on television once – I was glad it came back to me at that moment. After what seemed like for ever the attackers finally ran off and someone called an ambulance.

We were taken to May Day Hospital, where the doctor congratulated me on my quick thinking. I had pushed the tooth back into place so quickly that the nerve had knitted itself together again. But later in life the injury was to give me much pain and suffering; it still causes me distress today.

After the beating my friend and I looked as though we had been in a boxing match and had gone ten rounds with Muhammad Ali.

I often wonder if my attacker went on to be a wife-beater who also laid into his children. It wouldn't surprise me, as he had callously hit me, a defenceless nineteen-year-old girl, with such violent force.

The next day, Dardie decided to phone and report the attack to the newspaper that Caribbeans felt was the most sympathetic to them. We all gathered round as he dialled the number, wanting to hear their reaction to the story.

"I want to report a racist attack on my teenage daughter and her friend," said Dardie, with fury in his voice. "They were savagely beaten by a gang of racist thugs at a bowling alley, and no one came to their rescue." There was a silence, and the look on Dardie's face turned from anger to shock and disbelief. Then he slammed the receiver down in its cradle.

I looked towards him, trying to work out what had been said by the *Daily Mirror* journalist. "What did he say?" I asked anxiously through my swollen lips. "Are they going to put it in the paper?"

"You won't believe it," Dardie said with disappointment and dismay. "The journalist had the nerve to say, 'Tell me something new – these things happen every day!' That was the way it was in those days: unprovoked, violent racial attacks were an everyday occurrence. No justice was dished out that day.

I was so angry. Not angry with the newspaper or my attackers, but with myself. I should have known better. I had allowed myself to be lulled into a false sense of security and turned off my personal radar that detected danger. My defences were down and I had walked into a trap without realizing it.

This would never have happened before my spiritual experience. During that time I knew I could never trust a soul, so was always on guard, aware and ready to defend myself from those who hated me because of my colour.

But I didn't want to go back and resurrect the vicious, angry side of me that I had put to rest, so I decided to use this traumatic and violent attack as fuel to make me strong. I would keep no hatred locked up in my sad heart, for if I allowed that to happen, the perpetrators would have won. So I had to keep a smile on my face, to show I was a winner and nothing could break me.

But also I promised myself that was the last beating I would ever take. It would be a reminder of what could happen, if I ever let my guard down again. I had to be alert, always recognize signs, pick up the signals and deal with them appropriately.

I'm still on guard duty, even today!

CHAPTER TWENTY-ONE

On 23 September 1969, my twentieth birthday, I was happy as a humming-bird. I loved my birthdays and would announce each one to the world at least a month before it arrived. I still didn't celebrate with a party; my way of celebrating was to enjoy every second of my special day. My twenty years so far had been full of adventures, adversities and a growing sense that I had to find that intangible feeling of contentment if I were ever to be completely happy. Marmie always used to say to me, "You are never satisfied; you always want more. If you feel satisfied and contented, then you will be open and ready for what's right for you in life."

That was easier said than done. Why shouldn't I want to get more out of life? Why shouldn't I question and push the boundaries? And Marmie was one to talk; she had shown us by example to always reach for the sky, to keep moving forward and never give up. So if I followed her rules then I couldn't be contented just yet, because I myself didn't feel I had achieved any of my goals. Yes, I had gone through some traumas in my twenty-year journey and had overcome them. I was working in an office where I was respected and appreciated by most people. I'd influenced my colleagues' outlook on life by opening their minds and encouraging them to think differently. But something was missing in my life. I was not in my right place. I sometimes felt like a caged bird wanting to be freed.

I did feel liberated when I sang on stage with Dardie. That was the one time I felt that elusive sense of contentment. The music would be the rocket that blasted me into another dimension, a place without fear or anxiety, where I floated in a space that cushioned my soul. I was always disillusioned and sad when I had to come back to reality, but I realized I couldn't stay in that comfort zone for ever, I had to face real life.

In my world, time seemed to take for ever to complete its cycle, though I still felt that there was not going to be enough time to achieve all my ambitions and reach my final destiny. I was convinced I only had one more year to live, and there was too much to pack into the time I had allowed myself. My dream of becoming a bank manager would have to put on a spurt if it was to become a reality. But as I looked around the office at the people who were in charge, to a twenty-year-old they looked ancient, white and grey-haired. How could I possibly forge ahead and make my dream come true?

To make matters worse, the assistant manager, who had never quite taken to me, called me to his desk one day. What he said to me convinced me that I was not on the path that would take me to the valley of contentment. Although he made it obvious he didn't like me, I always tried to be pleasant to him, but I got the feeling that he thought I was too unconventional, and if he had had his way I would have been long gone from the office.

It was three o'clock on a Wednesday afternoon when the bombshell came. I remember it so well. The manager was away, so my nemesis took the opportunity to humiliate me. "Floella, take these papers over to the Bank of England for me right away," he said abrasively.

Now, every day around that time, papers were dispatched to the Bank of England, but never by the accounts staff. I said, with a note of surprise in my voice, "But sir, the messengers always take the papers over to the Bank."

"Well, I want you to do it today," he said irritably.

As I stared at him, my mind drifted back to the ugly-faced bullies I had confronted as a schoolgirl and I realized that bullies grow up and are everywhere, in all walks of life, spreading their poisonous venom. If they were happy souls, they wouldn't try to wield their power by spending precious time hurting others with their inconsiderate and cruel actions.

The fighting spirit rose up inside me as I faced yet another one of these ugly bullies and I felt compelled to stand up for myself. "I'm sorry, sir, but I am not a messenger. I think you should pick up the phone and call one of them to come and collect the papers as they usually do."

I looked at the podgy, spectacled, grey-haired man and wondered if my banking diploma or any of my qualifications meant anything to him. Or did he simply see me as someone beneath respect with no rights to equality? With obstacles like him in the way, it was going to take me a long time to break through the glass ceiling.

I walked back to my desk defiantly. I liked the messengers – they did a great job and were always pleasant to me. I would stop for a chat with them each day and we would have a laugh and a joke. But today I was in no laughing mood as I sat looking out of the window up on the ninth floor, wondering if it was time for me to escape.

CHAPTER TWENTY-TWO

A few weeks after the messenger incident, something showed itself that would change my life for ever. I had bought an evening paper on my way home from work. As I sat on the train, I opened it and an advert almost jumped off the page at me. It was not the usual sort of advert you saw in the evening paper, which was filled with columns of jobs for office workers.

When I look back – as I often do – I believe that tiny square of paper represented a pivotal moment in my life. It stood out on the page like a flashing neon sign.

"Singers and dancers wanted for a national musical tour. No theatrical experience necessary. Open auditions to be held at the Shaftesbury Theatre for one week."

I read it over and over again. I got the feeling it was a personal message to me, and somehow I felt compelled to go for the audition. I can sing, I thought to myself, I have been doing so for years with Dardie, and I can certainly dance. Marmie used to encourage me to learn all the latest dances; now was my chance to use these skills and take this opportunity. That night I thought about nothing else, and I decided I would definitely go for the audition.

I wanted to create an impression, so I thought I would dress like one of the Supremes, my favourite Motown girl group whose every movement Sandra and I knew. They always looked so glamorous in their pageboy-style wigs.

I owned a wig like theirs, so I secretly packed it in a bag together with a leopard-skin mini-dress, which was all the rage at that time, some brown leather knee-length boots and a pair of large round of earrings. I took them to work with me the next day. I didn't dare let Marmie know what I was up to – she would have gone mad.

"Working in a bank is a proper job, a job for life," she always said approvingly, after I had decided not to become a teacher.

Marmie had a great influence on what all her children did, and even though I sometimes deplored the control she had over us and the discipline we had to live by, deep down I knew it was out of love and because she wanted the best for us.

She had worked hard and made many sacrifices to get us to where we were. That took strength and will-power in the hostile environment we lived in. Yes, her love was tough love, coated with discipline, but it was the only way she knew to make our lives a success and to build our confidence so we could deal with the battles of life.

Because of her experiences of living with the uncertainty of Dardie and his music, Marmie believed that a career on stage was precarious, to say the least. It was certainly not part of her game plan for her children. So I dared not let my actions be known – well, not just yet. I planned that if I was successful at the audition, then I would cross that bridge.

As I sat at my desk that fateful morning I could think of nothing else. Just before my official lunch break, I made sure the coast was clear, then went into the toilet and changed into my glamorous theatrical outfit, complete with eyeshadow, rouge and extra lipstick. I felt like a star as I put my maxi coat on over the top, to disguise my unusual attire, and slipped out of the office. I took the underground train from Cannon Street to Tottenham Court Road and made my way to the Shaftesbury Theatre.

When I arrived, there was a small crowd of other hopefuls who had come for the audition. A friendly girl came up to me said, "Hello, welcome to the audition, my name's Daisy and I'm in charge backstage. I'll call you when it's your turn."

"Thank you," I said, and waited patiently until Daisy told me it was my turn to go on stage and show what I could do.

The huge, raked stage was painted black, and powerful spotlights shone onto it, almost blinding me. It was overwhelmingly vast, the biggest stage I had ever been on in my life. I stepped into the spotlight, putting my hands up

164

to shield to my eyes. I could just about make out a pianist sitting at an upright piano to my left.

Suddenly, a voice pierced the silence of the vast, cavernous, darkened auditorium. "What's your name, love?"

I peered into the darkness to try to make out who was there and, with as much confidence as I could muster, I shouted back, "Floella Benjamin."

"Hello, Floella. What are you going to sing for us?"

After much thought the night before, I had decided to sing one of the songs I loved singing with Dardie. "I'm going to sing 'I've Got You Under My Skin', in the key of F," I said proudly.

"Let's hear you, then, Floella," came the reply.

The pianist played the intro and I started in full swing. I felt myself zooming away into orbit, to the place I loved to be, enjoying every moment on stage as I belted out the song.

"Very good," said the mystery voice in the dark when I had finished. Because of the lights in my eyes, I still couldn't see who was out there, but whoever it was seemed to like me. "Can you move, love? Can you dance?" said the disembodied voice.

Can I move? Can I dance? I'll show you, I thought. The pianist struck up a lively tune and I showed them what I could do with every ounce of enthusiasm in my body. I gave it everything I had. But unfortunately my theatrical outfit was not prepared for these unexpected energetic gyrations. My unpinned pageboy wig flew off and went one way while I went the other. In an attempt to rescue the wig, I reached up to grab it – and as I did so my mini-dress rose almost up to my waist.

I quickly tried to regain my modesty as I heard wails of laughter coming back at me from the darkness. "That was quite a show, very amusing. Can you stay back and read for us, Floella?"

"Yes," I said, trying to cover up my embarrassment. I left the stage a little flustered, but exhilarated. Daisy gave me a script and told me to study the part of Abie Baby, which had to be spoken in an American accent. I had no problem with this, because Dardie used to take us to the cinema and encourage us to imitate American movie stars for our party pieces. So I went over the lines again and again with confidence while other hopefuls went through their paces on stage. Several of them came off in tears after hearing the dreaded call of "Next" from the darkness.

Suddenly I looked at my watch and realized the time. They say time flies when you're having fun, and the speed at which my lunch break had disappeared certainly proved that. I had been away from the office for far too long and I was getting rather worried, as I didn't want to give the assistant manager any ammunition to use against me. So I approached Daisy and explained, "I'm sorry to bother you, but I'm on my lunch break and I need to get back to work. Do you know how long it will be before I go back on?"

"I'll see what I can do," she said kindly. And when the next hopeful came off, Daisy announced, "Here is Floella again, to read for you."

I walked back onto the stage with my script, this time prepared for the bright lights.

"All right, Floella, let's hear you read the part of Abie Baby," said the voice.

I cleared my throat and delivered the lines. "Four score years and ten..." I spoke with feeling and clarity and tried to reach out to the whole theatre in my best American accent, using my imagination to become the character I was portraying.

"That was very good, Floella," said the voice in the darkness. "Just hang around for a while longer and we'll come back to you."

Well, that did it! I'd had enough of hanging around. I was not prepared to do just anything to get a part in the show at the risk of jeopardizing my job in the City. The casual attitude of the mystery voice made me feel as though he had no consideration for my circumstances – at that time it didn't occur to me that he had to see everyone before a choice was made. My big concern was to deglamorize myself and get back to work.

I was never shy about speaking out if I thought things were being done unfairly, and I felt this was one of those moments. So without a second thought, with my hand on my hip, I decided to give whoever it was out there a piece of my mind. "Excuse me," I said fearlessly, "I've got a proper job in a bank, you know. I've been here ages and I can't hang around any longer because I've got to get back to work. This is my lunch hour..."

No answer came back out from the stunned, silent darkness, so I continued with my protest. But as I stared into the void, I suddenly felt as though I was suspended in time and I had what might be described as a transcendental moment.

My mind was dramatically propelled by what felt like a cosmic force into a zone that allowed me to visualize my future. A future where I could excel and become the real me. I felt as though the journey I was about to take would lead me along a path to my true destiny, where I could find comfort in the arms of Britannia.

The audition was to be the launch pad from which I would be blasted off into my new life, for the show I was attempting to be part of was *Hair*, which was all about freedom of expression. Although people talked a lot about the sensational nude scene, *Hair* was more than just the show where members of the cast took off their clothes: it was a turning-point in musical theatre. The show was a new way of presenting realism on stage, a way for young people to try and change the thinking of the world. This is what I had been longing to do all my short life.

I began to get excited about what I might be able to achieve if I became an actress performing on a national stage and influencing people's thinking. Perhaps this was the sign I had been waiting for to bring contentment into my life. Even though I was auditioning only for a small part, I felt like a star, for to be part of the theatrical world was satisfaction in itself. I had experienced a little of what that meant when I'd sung with Dardie's band at gigs over the last few years, perfecting my performing skills and using the confidence Marmie had instilled in me.

I was well equipped to use my imagination. Dardie had always encouraged me to do so from the time I was a little girl back in Trinidad, during our bedtime stories, dressing-up and performing sessions. Like a magician I could conjure up different characters from the land of make-believe and put my heart and soul into them.

So I knew I could perform, because of the foundations and discipline my life was built on.

Nothing that was thrown at me would be too challenging. I was ready and I wanted to be part of this theatrical world more than ever. I was convinced at that moment that being in show business was going to be my new life.

But this musical *Hair* was not going to be an easy beginning. It meant I would have to be involved with people who led completely different lives from the one Marmie had forged for me. The age I was now living in was the hippie era of free love, where women's attitude to sex was liberated by "the pill", and where experimental drug-taking was normal practice. This was what had inspired *Hair*, and the actors had to convince the audience they were watching realism, which was why the producers were looking for people with little or no theatrical experience, like me.

I was going to be among individuals who were prepared to push the boundaries of what was considered acceptable, in a groundbreaking show so controversial it had almost been banned because of its content. I was sure Dardie would see beyond all that and give me his blessing, as well as all the encouragement I needed to follow in his footsteps into the world of show business.

Marmie, on the other hand, was going to find it hard to accept the fact that her daughter wanted to be in a show associated with what she would call unashamed indecency. Her stern face appeared before me, her words about having dignity and respect for myself resonated in my head. I knew that selling this dramatic change in direction to her was going to be difficult, to say the least! But I had to find a way to convince her to allow me to set off on a course of discovery, like an explorer going on a journey to a new world. However, for her to share the vision I had of my future, I would have to reassure her that I would keep intact the principles, integrity, beliefs and values she had instilled in me. Because of her influence, I would enter this new phase of my life knowing I had to do it my way rather than be swept along with the crowd. I would not be a sheep but a shepherd.

At that moment, standing on the stage, I felt I had the power within me to take that quantum leap. I was quietly convinced I was on the right track, in the right place to start off in this new career, because even though I came back from my cosmic trip, back to earth, where time had not moved on, there was still no sound coming out of the stunned darkness. Whoever it was out there must have been under a spell, or completely aghast at my impertinence at speaking out the way I had. Perhaps they found me spirited and feisty, the way they wanted the characters in the show to be. Whatever the reason, I seized the opportunity to set out my terms and conditions with an air of confidence

171

and determination. It was the way I intended to continue in the exciting and glamorous world of show business, which, ever since seeing that fateful advert in the evening paper, I somehow knew I was about to enter.

So with a smile on my face, joy in my voice and happiness in my soul, I announced to the listener in the darkness, "...so if you do want me to be in your show, you had better tell me right now. Oh and by the way, I want thirty pounds a week and I'm not taking my clothes off!"

Afterword

Being a teenager can cause anxiety, fear, loss of confidence and uncertainty about what the future holds. That's how I sometimes felt when I was a teenager, but I have discovered that I was not alone. In this book, a follow-up to *Coming to England*, which I wrote over fifteen years ago, I felt compelled to talk about the many issues – emotional, psychological and in some cases physical – that young people have to deal with no matter what culture they are from. That said, coming from a culturally diverse background also had its added challenges. What I do know is that everything that has happened to me over the last sixty years has been for a reason, even though I haven't always realized it at the time. But now, as I stand on the summit of the mountain I have climbed and look back into the deep valley of experience, it's like looking through a telescope which brings my life closely into focus. Every minute of my journey has been woven into a rich tapestry of memories which I hope will give others inspiration, solace and comfort.

As a descendant of enslaved people, I often glance back respectfully at my history, but I also constantly move forward with a mission to pave a path for future generations, and ensure the memory of my ancestors stays alive and is celebrated.

To know and understand history is vital to achieving peace of mind and planning for the future. Marmie and Dardie started me off on that road of discovery and I couldn't have flourished without them guiding me onto the right track. I have to thank my sisters, Sandra and Cynthia, and my brothers, Lester, Ellington and Roy Junior, for being part of both my wonderful childhood and my development into a happy teenager. Without their love, support and encouragement I wouldn't be who I am today.

Marmie and Dardie were the best parents any child could hope for when it came to opening our minds and giving all their six children the ability to see the bigger picture. It's a gift I treasure and share, not just with my own children, Aston and Alvina, but with all the young people I meet. Part of that gift is sharing this, my teenage story.

This story is also a record of an aspect of Caribbean and British history, which is often forgotten and could die with the pioneers who came to Britain and lived through a time when they were made to feel unworthy.

My burning desire is to make people feel as though they belong and are part of a long history which stretches back four centuries. Dardie's colonial boss told him that taking his children to Britain was foolhardy and would fail. But Dardie swore his children would be successful in their new homeland, and how right he was, because we all made him and Marmie very proud. I just wish they had not both passed away before I became a baroness.

I sometimes wonder what the slave masters of my forefathers would think of descendants like me documenting a part of British history in the twenty-first century!

I must thank my dearest husband, Keith, the love I hoped for, who protects me and guides me through life. Also Walker Books, for allowing me to tell this treasured part of my story.

Before I leave you, I want to share some of my philosophy with you. Remember to live your life to the full, giving with the joy and passion you would like to receive. Never become or see yourself as a victim, even when others go out of their way to make you feel like one. Keep on thinking, "I am worthy; it's not my fault."

Never hold any bitterness or resentment in your heart, because that is another way of being turned into a victim and letting others have a hold over you. Move forward and blossom by using your experiences to make you stronger.

Your teenage years may be the most tumultuous period you go through. They certainly were for me, but I made it through and have lived to tell the tale.

Finally, wherever you go and whatever you do, remember there is always someone who loves you ... and that's me ... Floella xx

COMING to England

"Belonging is the most important thing."

COMING to England
an autobiography
by
Floella Benjamin

First published in 1995, this touching autobiography is a unique record of the experience of immigration from one of Britain's best-loved television personalities.

When Floella Benjamin first came to England from Trinidad in 1960, she hadn't seen her parents for fifteen months. At first, her joy at being reunited with them overcomes the shock at her new surroundings in cold, hostile London but when she starts school she is upset by the taunting and rejection she faces. Determined to survive, she realizes that the only way is to strive to be twice as good as everyone else.

www.floellabenjamin.com